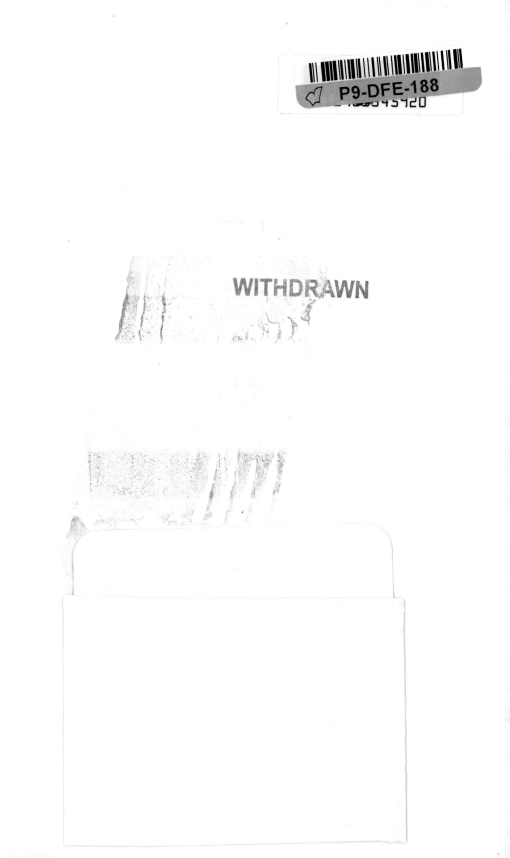

The NEW IMPERIALISTS

MARK LEIBOVICH

Prentice Hall Press

Library of Congress Cataloging-in-Publication Data

Leibovich, Mark.
    The new imperialists / Mark Leibovich.
        p.   cm.
    Includes index.
    ISBN 0-7352-0317-2
    1. Businessmen—United States. 2. Executives—United States. 3. Computer
industry—United States—Management—Case studies. 4. Computer software
industry—United States—Case studies. 5. Ellison, Larry. Bezos, Jeffrey. Chambers,
John, 1949- 8. Gates, Bill, 1955- 9. Case, Stephen McConnell. Title.
    HC102.5.A2 L385 2001
    338.7'61004'09273—dc21   2002051047

Acquisitions Editor: *Tom Power*
Production Editor: *Eve Mossman*
Page Design/Layout: *Robyn Beckerman*

©2002, Learning Network Direct, Inc., publishing as Prentice Hall Press

Printed in the United States of America

10 9 8 7 6 5 4 3 2 1

ISBN 0-7352-0317-2

ATTENTION: CORPORATIONS AND SCHOOLS

Prentice Hall Press books are available at quantity discounts with bulk purchase for educational, business, or sales promotional use. For information, please write to: Prentice Hall Special Sales, 240 Frisch Court, Paramus, New Jersey 07652. Please supply: title of book, ISBN, quantity, how the book will be used, date needed.

Prentice Hall Press Paramus, NJ 07652

http://www.phpress.com

In memory of two dear friends:
my grandfather, Samuel C. Brownstein,
and my brother, Phil Leibovich.

For Nell

CONTENTS

ACKNOWLEDGMENTS

Like being a CEO, writing a book is a lonely job whose fate rests heavily with the people who surround the venture (and that's about where the comparisons end). This project was many things—a pleasure, a challenge, a dream, an ordeal and, ultimately, a collaboration. I am ever-grateful to the hundreds who provided such a rich quilt of anecdotes, memories and insights for me to work with. Any errors of fact or interpretation are entirely my own.

My special thanks:

- To *The Washington Post*—for the daily kick and osmosis benefit of working there; to Don Graham, Bo Jones, Len Downie and Steve Coll for supporting the kinds of ambitious projects that would become this book.

  To my pals and mentors in the Post's financial section, present and past: especially (in random order) Nell Henderson, Larry Roberts, Peter Goodman, Tracy Grant, Jonathan Krim, Justin Gillis, Mike Mills, Rajiv Chandrasekeran, John Burgess, Pete Behr, Jerry Knight, Shannon Henry, John Schwartz, Leslie Walker, Alec Klein, Fred Barbash, David Streitfeld, Glenn Kessler, and David Ignatius. To Richard Drezen, whose dogged research saved me immeasurable time; to Mickey Trimarchi, Mike Stuntz and everyone on the financial copy desk who saved me great embarassment; to Henry Wytko and Joyce Fekkak in the Washington Post travel office who saved me huge hassles; and to Eric Lieberman in the Post's legal department who saved me from fates I don't like to think about.

To Joe Elbert, Linda Salazar, Giuliana Nakashima, Michael Williamson and the Post photo department. To Glenn Frankel and the ever-hospitable staff of the Washington Post Magazine ("the Bunker"), and to the assorted lunch buddies, mentors, and resident masters who make this such a creative place to wander: Paul Farhi, David Segal, Frank Ahrens, Bill Hamilton, Steve Fainaru, Kevin Merida, Anne Hull, Nicole Arthur, Hanna Rosin, Joel Garreau, Mary Hadar, Tom Wilkinson, David Finkel, Peter Perl, and David Maraniss, among others.

- To the subjects of this book who, after initial reservations, were all more than generous with their time. I shudder to calculate the CEO man-hours that have been lost to this project—and could this explain the technology downturn? Bill Gates, Larry Ellison, Jeff Bezos, Steve Case, and John Chambers sat for, in most cases, multiple interviews, phone conversations, and follow-up e-mails. They opened their companies to me, made their families available, and, perhaps their biggest sacrifice, furnished embarrassing childhood photos of themselves. The profiles in this book are much, much richer for their participation.

- To the gatekeepers at each company, who were (as PR-types like to say), "so nice to *work* with." Mark Murray, Keith Hodson and Corey duBrowa at Microsoft, Jennifer Glass and Carolyn Balkenhol at Oracle, Bill Curry and Lizzie Allen at Amazon, Kathy Bushkin and Trish Primrose at AOL, and Kent Jenkins and Chris Peacock at Cisco.

- To a kitchen cabinet of friends, sources, and industry rabbis who made various and vital contributions—from reading portions of the manuscript, to lending ideas (and indulging mine), coining phrases, truth-squading tales, opening their guest rooms, sharing meals and essentially performing the odd jobs of friendship that make a huge difference in endeavors like this: Shelby Barnes, Paul Saffo, Michael Maccoby, Kara Swisher, David Plotz, Mark Andreessen, Matt Glickman, Scott Thurm, Michael Kolbrener, John Sidgmore, Jim Boyd, Ned Zeman, Joshua Weinstein, Zippy Zeitlin, Pedro Martinez, Doug Okun, Ken Novack, Mike Wilson, Bill Whyman, Ellen Hancock, Adam Stein, and many others.

- To my agent, Rafe Sagalyn, and Claire Smith, of the Sagalyn Literary Agency, for their judgment, savvy, and kindness, and for believing in The New Imperialists at a time when "The New Economy Story" was about as hot in publishing as it was on Wall Street. Without them, this book would likely never exist.

- To the staff at Prentice Hall Press—Tom Power, Debora Yost, Yvette Romero, and Eve Mossman—for taking this project on, and for seeing it through with such patience and care.

- The Best for Last Categories: To my boss, Jill Dutt, whose support, patience, and passion through this saga was both an inspiration and a godsend. And my editor, T.A. Frail, a New Imperialist hero, who "became one with" my stories to a degree that editors rarely do. His brilliance, trust, and humor not only made this possible, but also a blast.

- To my family, in its assorted units—Pop and Betty, Mom and Ted, Sklor and Larry, Jack and Barbara—for their love and support. And a special snog for Val Tomkins.

- Above all, to my wife, Meri Kolbrener, and daughter, Nell, who make waking up and coming home the best parts of the day.

PREFACE

By Paul Saffo

Innovation is irrational. Most inventions flop, most start-ups fail, and all but a tiny fraction of would-be entrepreneurs end up working in obscurity for someone else. As scientist and innovator Danny Hillis observes, "in the natural world, the word for innovation is mutation, and mostly it is fatal."

But, occasionally, this huge, wasteful innovation machine delivers something new that changes the way we live. And when this happens, there is usually a single driven individual linked to the life-changing novelty. Bill Gates and the PC, Steve Case and online services, Jeff Bezos and online shopping, Larry Ellison and relational databases, John Chambers and Internet plumbing—all of them are as much symbols as they are business imperialists.

Like all symbols, no small part of these associations are pure myth. For example, Bill Gates didn't invent the PC; he didn't even write DOS, the predecessor to Windows. All this was done by others, and Bill is simply the poster boy for the personal computer revolution. But all myths have a grain of truth, and the truth in this case goes to the heart of why these titans fascinate us.

Innovation fascinates us, but we also fear it. Innovation is welcomed after it happens, but fiercely resisted when it is under-way. When push comes to shove, we really prefer to keep things as they are. In the words of Mark Twain, "I am all for progress; it is change I object to." These innovators fascinate us because, against all odds, they are turning our world upside down. They are cajol-ing us to buy into their vision of the future—and literally, for it is of course our money that finances their enterprises. Bill is at best a mediocre technologist, but he is also an astonishing business genius, adept at overcoming all obstacles that might derail his particular vision.

Meanwhile, we wrap other myths atop our misunderstanding. Larry Ellison the person may be an arrogant jackass, but Ellison the icon is the embodiment of the hopes that drew Europeans to the new world a century ago. It is a myth embodied in his last name, itself the invention of the relative who reared him, chosen as an homage to the famous port of entry, Ellis Island. Jeff Bezos' self-effacing charm in the face of wealth and power makes him the son every mother wished she had reared, a mix of Charles Lindberg and Will Rogers. And John Chambers is the quintiessential Captain of Industry—soft-spoken, southern-gentlemanly, steady-helmed and very, very tough. I have watched him bring a room of Fortune 20 CEOs to hushed silence and turn them into a bunch of breathless, heart-throbbing groupies, hanging off his every word.

With all this baggage, it is little surprise that we know remarkably little about these world changers. Until now. Against all odds, the author has penetrated both the myths and the publicity bubble to deliver an intimate look at these individuals and what makes them tick. Despite Bezos' oft-repeated claims, Amazon was no "happy accident," but the result of relentless thinking and even more relentless work. And Steve Case's refusal to talk about his personal life may not have cracked when Leibovich interviewed him, but the myriad friends and former business colleagues Mark tracked down did. The result is a view of Case that will surprise even industry insiders.

This book is at once a time capsule of a revolution in the making, and a rare look into what really drives successful innovators to change our world. It is thus an invaluable read for anyone trying to make sense of the information revolution swirling around us, but I'll also bet that more than a few executives will pick it up and finally begin to understand what makes the Titan they work for tick.

INTRODUCTION

Bill Gates was just kidding—but "just kidding" can be dangerous when you're Bill Gates. This had the makings of a small international incident.

He was sitting in his office with Steve Ballmer, Microsoft's chief executive and Gates's best friend. They were discussing a burden that, it's safe to assume, most friends never have to worry about. When foreign leaders visit Seattle, they often seek an audience with Gates. But since Ballmer replaced him as CEO, Gates has started delegating some of the meetings to Ballmer—to the obvious disappointment of some visitors, who would rather meet with Microsoft's founder, the World's Richest Man. How, I wondered, did Gates and Ballmer divide up these meetings without making the dignitaries feel slighted.

"I get the heads of state of countries," Gates explained. But with a few rare exceptions.

"Mauritius," Ballmer said smirking, "I was able to handle on my own."

"I was worried about it though," Gates said.

They chuckled together, a tidy moment for me to capture in a story I was writing about Gates and Ballmer for *The Washington Post* in December 2000. But a few weeks later, just before the article was to come out, Microsoft PR chief Mark Murray became concerned about Mauritius. The exchange could be insulting to the citizens and leaders of the tiny island nation east of Madagascar.

Did I really have to use this part of the conversation in the story?

Yes, I said. Mauritius was staying in. Murray asked again, a little more plaintively. But after a few minutes of back and forth on the matter, our phone call ended. We published the Mauritius exchange. And, somehow, Microsoft survived.

These are the episodes that yield periodic reminders that the world has changed. The recognition comes in little snatches, as when it suddenly occurs to you: *We are living in an age where people have straight-faced discussions about two slobs possibly insulting Mauritius with a throwaway interlude from Redmond, Washington.*

I have written about the technology industry for six years, first in Silicon Valley during the cultural invasion of the Internet, then in Washington at both the peak and depths of the sector's boom-and-bust ride. It has been, and continues to be, a great, important and wacky story, rife with money, ego, conflict, daily doses of strategic intrigue, and real-life impact. But sometimes, the heady weirdness of it all would pinch me.

Like when I would notice that the schedule of America Online's Steve Case matter-of-factly included breakfast with the King of Jordan and a briefing at a congressional retreat; that Oracle's founder Larry Ellison had casually blown off a meeting with Tony Blair; that Amazon's Jeff Bezos beat out Alan Greenspan and Jiang Zemin to be Time's Man of the Year, and that Cisco's John Chambers was discussing prospective administration jobs with officials from both the Gore and Bush campaigns.

Who were these men? They seemed to come from Oz, a cohort of sudden tycoons who thrived in an anarchic economic world where multinational corporations increasingly have supplanted national governments as sources of power. Modern imperialism is a corporate, global imperialism—a world ruled by transnational executives with extraordinary influence not only over business issues but also things like immigration, environmental and trade policy. Likewise, today's imperialists are the audacious breed of computing entrepreneurs who have made ubiquity their corporate objectives, with slogans like "A Computer on Every Desktop" and "Get Big Fast." They are the generals of the networked world's ruling empires—and this will define them in history whether the so-called New Economy is recalled as a revolutionary phenomenon, or a delusional one.

These New Imperialists—Gates of Microsoft, Case of AOL, Ellison of Oracle, Bezos of Amazon, and Chambers of Cisco—became the contemporary faces of Capitalist ambition, or arrogance, or both. They were never content to do something so utterly mundane as "build" successful companies. They needed to expand, expand, and expand through the boundlessness of cyberspace and into fresh global markets to find out exactly what they were capable of, what they could get away with, and how far they could go.

To some extent, all of them battled social or developmental problems when they were kids: Gates and Bezos were small for their ages, precocious and subject to bullying from other children; Ellison had difficulty telling the truth and Case was a loner; Chambers battled dyslexia and for a time believed he was stupid. In another time and place, all five could have landed in anonymity. Or, worse, in middle-management. Instead, they found solace in the emerging frontier of computing—purpose in a box—where they would seize slices of virtual turf and build them into commercial superpowers.

They became, in digital age parlance, "brands" unto themselves—Gates: the prickly alpha-nerd; Ellison: billionaire bad boy, playboy, perpetual boy; Bezos, giggly shopkeeper of electronic commerce; Case, cunningly pragmatic leader of cunningly pragmatic AOL; Chambers, messianic Southern preacher of net-worked possibility. And when the history of the digital age is writ-ten—beyond the dazzle of new technology, the titillation of overnight wealth, and the cautionary tales of subsequent loss—the story can largely be distilled to the lives of these five men.

Which, beyond the most superficial of their "brand" per-sonae, are lives that we know very little about.

It's not for lack of exposure or attention. These captains have become standard magazine cover fodder, the subject of countless profiles, interviews. Each is backed by sophisticated public rela-tions teams, speechwriters, and message-mavens, many of whom came from similar jobs in the political and advertising world. As with the companies they run, the brands of these titans are scrubbed, protected, and sold aggressively. Indeed, I had read exhaustively about these men over the years, interviewed them, studied them and wrote about them many times.

Yet I never had any real clue about what formed the desper-ate edges to their ambitions. What gave them the savvy and con-fidence to consolidate such staggering wealth and power? What childhood episodes, conflicts, and relationships whetted their appetites for dominance as adults? And what, simply, was it like to inhabit their celebrity lives today—to sit with them in their offices, in their homes, in a restaurant?

I set out to learn their fuller stories, as far from the cliches, PR-machines, and quick-time assumptions as I could get. I wanted to hear the tales that, at the hyper velocities of Internet time, there was so little time to find, let alone to tell and to reflect on. Over 14 months in 2000 and 2001, I interviewed roughly 400 people who have known Gates, Case, Ellison, Bezos, and Chambers best—parents, siblings, neighbors, teachers, former bosses, long-time associates, employees, and adversaries. I spent hours with the subjects themselves, discussing formative—and largely unknown—

topics from their pasts. They were all expansive, thoughtful and reflective, to varying degrees (Bezos being the most, Case the least). The results comprise the five portraits that follow, shorter versions of which appeared as part of a series in *The Washington Post* in 2000 and early 2001.

By definition, entrepreneurs are bold figures, driven, often meglomaniacal. The kings of the Industrial Age were up-from-nothing legends: John D. Rockefeller, the son of a peddler in Richford, N.Y., spent part of his adolescence working as a clerk in a produce firm. Andrew Carnegie, the son of a Scottish weaver, emigrated to Pittsburgh at 12 and took a job in a cotton mill. Henry Ford was born on a farm in Dearborn, Michigan, and went to work as a machinist at 16. For them, growing up poor was an experience both searing and transforming.

In contrast, the New Imperialists emerged from the serene, TV-entranced and non-Vietnam-going neighborhoods of the 1960s and 1970s, a world in which the most common form of adversity was boredom. They were all raised with big expectations and in wealthy suburban families, with the exception of Ellison (though not to the degree that he has often claimed). Absent any pressing material needs, they nonetheless developed a hunger to dominate the world. I wanted to find out what possessed them to do this, to better understand their characters, psyches and, in some cases, their demons.

Besides the figures I profiled here, I considered a few others, but dismissed them for various reasons: Andy Grove of Intel is the undisputed pioneer of computer chip-making, which underpins so much high-tech innovation; but Grove retired three years ago, and has little to do with the day-to-day operations of Intel today. Steve Jobs of Apple is ferociously bold and has solid inventors' cachet; but for as iconic as Apple has been under him, the company is still a niche player in personal computing, hardly dominant. Michael Dell of Dell founded one of the most successful PC-makers in the world, but his historic credential is more process-oriented than visionary—he developed and mastered a mail-order sales model. In a broader sense, it's possible, if not likely, for a PC-user to have no experience at all with an Apple or Dell product.

This is not true for the realms of the New Imperialists. They came to rule key sectors so fully that it would be difficult, if not impossible, for most citizens to go through a week without some contact with their products. Nearly all personal computer users rely on Microsoft—to a point where if the company changes in its interface, its pricing or its privacy code, it will likely have more real effect on the lives of people in, say, Mauritius, than nearly any policy decision that George W. Bush could make. If you use an automatic teller machine, make a credit card purchase, or need employee benefits information, you're data is likely being "managed" by Oracle's software products—a reliance that will grow exponentially as humankind creates more new information in the next three years than it has in the rest of its history, according to researchers at the University of California. If you want to buy something online, Amazon is the obvious first place to look for most things—and the transaction will no doubt proceed by way of some Cisco hardware tool within the "plumbing" of the Internet. If you're a media consumer, you will inevitably encounter some AOL-controlled outlet—its dominant online service, its CNN programs, Warner Brothers films, or *Sports Illustrated*, *Time*, or *People* magazines, the ones with the AOL disks stuck inside.

While there have always been expansive global companies—the Coca Colas, McDonald's, Standard Oils—these New Imperialists achieved their dominance seemingly overnight, and to a degree that has exploded any previous notion of commercial scope and scale. Moreover, their wired age goals go beyond mere geographic expansion; they incorporate a kind of lifestyle imperialism in which traditional lines of media and commerce are constantly being pushed. Microsoft no longer just wants to provide the software for the "Computer on Every Desktop." It also wants to make the software that powers your game consoles, set-top TV boxes, and a range of products and services on the Internet; just as AOL wants to meld its TV shows with its online channels with its magazine content with its movie promos with any mix-and-match of media "convergence" you could imagine; just as Amazon wants to lure customers who shop on cellular devices, perhaps the same devices whose communiques might travel by way of Cisco products made for wireless networks.

Yes, several "Old Economy" companies have also expanded their offerings to suit broader lifestyle tastes—McDonalds, for instance, stretched from hamburgers and Cokes into salads, desserts, and breakfasts. But what distinguishes the New Imperialists is their quest for total ubiquity, a sense of manifest destiny that is captured in America Online's corporate mantra, "AOL Anywhere." It's a poignant statement, not just of one company's voracious aims, but of the kinds of boundless goals that the networked economy now allows for.

Where does a person acquire the hunger to be "anywhere?" On cell phones, on dashboards, on AOL-TV, in Brazil? I set upon gathering data to deepen and expand on the too-glossy records of their lives. The more I learned, the more it reinforced my premise for this project: that in order to fully comprehend one of the most transforming and tumultuous eras in American history, it's vital to know where its leaders came from, and what they've grown up to be.

CHAPTER ONE

LARRY ELLISON

Is It Really True?

Larry Ellison, the world's second-richest man, was entertaining friends aboard his 243-foot yacht off Capri when another yacht caught his attention. A mere 200-foot yacht, belonging to Microsoft co-founder Paul Allen. The world's third-richest man.

As Allen's yacht set out on a twilight cruise to the village of Positano, Ellison instructed his captain to rev his boat's three engines to full speed. Within minutes, his craft overtook Allen's at 40 mph, leaving a huge and sudden wake that sent Allen and his passengers staggering across the deck. Ellison and his friends were belly-laughing as his yacht returned to its anchorage.

A spokesperson for Allen declined to comment on the episode, which occurred at the end of August 2000. "It was an adolescent prank," said Ellison, who was 56 at the time. "I highly recommend it."

This is the sort of thing that makes Silicon Valley's most successful entrepreneur such an easy caricature. He is the founder and chief executive of Oracle Corp., the world's second-biggest software company and—as businesses shift their functions online—one formidably positioned to profit from the Internet's expansion. Ellison's net worth, which is tied closely to the performance of Oracle stock, has ranged between $20 billion to $80 billion since 1999, and has sporadically surpassed Bill Gates's.

But when Ellison receives attention, it's often for reasons irrelevant to his corporate bona fides. In a three-month period in the middle of 2000—a period in which I happened to be writing about him—Ellison made the following news: In June, he admitted that Oracle had hired a private investigator to snoop on a pro-Microsoft Corp. trade organization in Washington (this snoop work included stealing the pro-Microsoft group's trash). A few days later Ellison's longtime deputy, Ray Lane, left the company in a public spat. Ellison continued a long-running battle with authorities at San Jose Airport for the right to violate its 11 P.M. curfew with his Gulfstream V jet. A Florida man alleged in a lawsuit that Ellison stiffed him out of a $700,000 commission when he bought a $10-million yacht. A former housekeeper was accused of stealing his Rolex. His McLaren F1 sports car was reportedly issued a fake smog certificate.

That was just one summer.

Ellison's swamping of Paul Allen's yacht occurred in August. While it was not reported in the news media, Ellison's friends told the story relentlessly, to the point where it became an instant Silicon Valley legend. "It is great to create these artificial confrontations that are motivational," Ellison told me a few weeks after he'd returned from the Mediterranean. "No doubt they are childish. I don't dispute that for a second."

By the way, he said, you should have seen the looks on the faces of Paul Allen's friends as they tumbled across the deck. Their dinner went flying. Their wine spilled all over their clothes. "We destroyed their *wa*," Ellison said, explaining that *wa* is the Japanese word for tranquility. He laughed as he said this, a pitched, girlish giggle.

No more than 30 seconds later, Ellison was wondering why his sweeping impact on the world had been so obscured. Oracle's database software automates the taken-for-granted functions of modern commerce: It provides unseen tools that track data in automated teller machines, ease credit card transactions, and underpin online commerce. Few people know how to use Oracle's software, but many encounter it in some indirect fashion every day.

Ellison, who founded Oracle in 1977, is both the ultimate Silicon Valley entrepreneur and its consummate outsider. He typifies the extremes of the technology industry: its wealth, brilliance, and speed as well as its ego, hype, and ruthlessness. But he did not emerge from the privileged environment that nourished so many New Economy ambitions, the old-money lineage of, say, his chosen foil, Gates. "William Gates the Third," corrects Ellison, deriding the only man richer than he.

Born to an unwed 19-year-old in Manhattan, Lawrence Joseph Ellison was adopted at 9 months by distant relatives in Chicago. Louis Ellison was a Russian Jew who had changed his long surname to commemorate his passage through Ellis Island, a newcomer seeking acceptance and self-renewal. These themes he conveyed to his adopted son by assuring him that he would always fail.

Beyond his outward refinement—his Armani suits, his Beverly Hills nose job—Larry Ellison's approach to business betrays a raw desperation. "I can't imagine anything worse than failing," he said. His willingness to say this also sets him apart. "For as competitive as it is in Silicon Valley, there's this idea that everyone should be playing like it's all a friendly chess match," says Marc Benioff, a former Oracle executive and an Ellison protege. "Larry doesn't think this for a second. He thinks of himself as a samurai warrior."

In late 1999, Benioff left Oracle after thirteen years to start Salesforce.com, an online software service for sales operations. Ellison gave his blessing, plus a $2-million investment. He joined the board.

Six months later, Benioff learned that Oracle had launched a competing business. He demanded that Ellison resign his board seat. Ellison refused.

"It would sound a lot cooler if you kicked me off," Ellison said, according to Benioff. "It would be a better story to tell my friends."

Ellison's version: "I said, 'Marc, I'm surprised you don't want to throw me off. It would get you more publicity, and that's what you've been using me for all along.'"

Both men agreed that Ellison, while resigning, quibbled over the Salesforce.com stock options he felt entitled to.

THE FOG OF DECEIT

Ellison places two fingers on his tongue and makes like he's gagging. The topic: high-tech leaders who trumpet their enterprises as Crusades for Good—as if they had nothing to do with riches and conquest. His rapid-fire speech slows to a cadence of disdainful sarcasm:

"Oh, well, the reason we're doing software here at Oracle is because someday children will use this software, and we wouldn't want to leave a single child behind. If I could just make the world a better place, what I really care about is making the world a better place, and that's why I'm doing this. And all my money's going to go to medical research so we can help people who are sick."

At which point he gags himself again.

"People say this and get away with it," he says, patting his temples with the tips of his long and manicured fingers. "I can't deal with the fog of deceit."

Deceit is a complicated notion with Ellison. He's been accused of practicing it in many forms: exaggerating the capabilities of Oracle products, embellishing the meanness of his boyhood neighborhood, and misleading people about the academic degrees he has earned.

At the same time, the rough transparency of Ellison's bravado flouts the public relations obsession of his industry. I asked him when he knew the Internet would be big. A soft, fat question.

It was in the early 1990s, he said. He was visiting his daughter's kindergarten class, and he saw all the 5-year-olds using it. The PR woman who was monitoring my interview nodded reassuringly.

By the way, his daughter's teacher was "an incredibly pretty, single young lady," said Ellison, who has been thrice divorced. "Really, I never saw a kindergarten teacher look like that before." The image of toddlers in cyberspace was lost. The PR woman's smile was frozen.

Ellison continued. It was parents' day in school. "So, dad comes into kindergarten class. . . . I said to my daughter, 'Megan, who's that?' 'That's Miss Baker, Dad.' I said, 'Good deal.' She was also the head of the computer lab." Ellison mentions Miss Baker's full name several times, quite clearly trying to get his esteem for her in the newspaper.

Ellison is sitting in his eleventh-floor office at Oracle, a bright, large, and obsessively cleaned place decorated with Japanese paintings and ceramics. His is one of those faces that is both homely and handsome at the same time, with cheeks worn red from sailing and busy brown eyes that turn soft when he smiles, squinty when he talks. His repaired nose sits in triangular symmetry with his long and bearded jaw.

No fan of tech-casual dress, Ellison wears a charcoal gray sports jacket over a black turtleneck. He rests his size-12 feet on a glass table. He is 6 foot 1, trim, and somewhat body-obsessed. He often refers to people in terms of their size—"small," "huge," a "giant"—and shares a personal trainer with former San Francisco 49ers quarterback Joe Montana. If Ellison misses a workout, he is prone to vocal self-loathing.

"To Larry, so much of his power comes from physical fitness," says Jenny Overstreet, his longtime assistant until she retired at age 35 in 1996. He talks about how his body feels and looks, Overstreet says, "like a woman saying, 'My thighs are fat today.'"

Ellison greets visitors to his office with a soft but firm handshake and a courtly bow. He breaches no rule of decorum except that he is unfailingly late. Unapologetically late—and not a little bit late.

"Every time we'd go to lunch, he'd be thirty, sixty, ninety minutes late," said Stuart Feigin, Oracle's fifth employee, who calls his former boss "the late Larry Ellison." Ellison was 90 minutes late for an interview I did with him in October 2000. He did not apologize, he only explained: He was in a meeting. He has a hard time getting out of meetings. He is "somewhat reassured" that two of the people he most admires, Winston Churchill and Bill Clinton, were and are habitually late.

Still, there are legions of Ellison lateness tales to suggest an edgier character. At an Oracle-sponsored demonstration for U.S. Defense Department clients in Herndon, Virginia, a group of high-level Pentagon officials waited 45 minutes until Ellison pulled up in a limousine. He kept Philippines President Fidel Ramos waiting more than an hour in his San Francisco mansion. When Ellison arrived, Ramos waited 15 minutes more while Ellison changed clothes.

I experienced something similar on the one previous time I'd met Ellison. In November of 1997, Ellison came to Washington to attend a White House dinner for Chinese premier Jiang Zemin. He was scheduled to come to *The Washington Post* for lunch with a group of editors and reporters, but he canceled at the last minute for reasons never made clear. Instead, a group of us were invited to interview him at the Hay-Adams Hotel, across from the White House. Our delegation included *Post* technology editor John Burgess, reporter Rajiv Chandrasekaran, and me. We were met in the lobby at the appointed hour—3 P.M.—by Keith Hodson, an

Oracle public relations man. Hodson told us that Ellison was running behind schedule, about 30 minutes. We killed time by strolling around a park across the street. After 30 minutes, Hodson led us back to the hotel and upstairs to Ellison's suite, where we took seats on couches and waited for Ellison. And waited. It was clear Ellison was in an adjoining bedroom, behind a closed door.

Hodson kept apologizing. He also mentioned this was his last day at Oracle, and that he'd taken a new job—at Microsoft—that would start the following week, but could we please not mention this to Ellison.

After 15 minutes, Ellison's door opened and a willowy and fit young woman with light brown hair walked out. "I'm Melanie," she said, offering us something to drink. Ellison's girlfriend. She stood around awkwardly. Finally, after another 15 minutes, Burgess told Hodson we had to leave. Hodson knocked on Ellison's door, opened it slightly and whispered something, then returned, saying it would be another minute. Five minutes later, we headed to the door—and no sooner did Ellison stick his head out the bedroom door and yell, "Melanie, where's my belt?" Melanie returned to the bedroom, then Ellison strode out in a pressed charcoal suit, buckling his belt, ready.

We are fortunate he came out at all, it turned out. Numerous engagements with Ellison are lost to his caprice. As a general rule, his scheduling commitments come with an eleventh-hour proviso: Larry Permitting. He has a 5-year-old's attention span when he's bored and an ability to delve deep if he cares to. It suits him to running a company on Internet time. His mind can pinball from topic to topic and focus when necessary. He also tends to say whatever is on his mind.

"I'm not trying to figure out what would serve me best in print," Ellison said on the subject of doing and saying exactly what he feels like doing and saying. "It's very interesting. Some people who like me would say there's a high degree of integrity. Other people would see it as incredibly self-destructive. Then, the third group would say, 'I can't believe he's saying that,' he's just an asshole."

He says the first two groups would be right.

Rest assured, Ellison wants to be loved, more and more as he gets older. "The reason you want to be loved," he said, "is because you want to love yourself and feel self-esteem."

Does he feel sufficiently loved? "No, of course not." He's learned this over time and struggle (therapy? "None, nada. I tried marriage counseling once"), and he hates that he's perceived as mean, ruthless. "I don't think mean and ruthless people are loved." He has tried to improve, he said earnestly, almost plaintively. He *is* improving.

LARRYLAND

When I met with Ellison in his office in the fall of 2000, he invited me to return to California the following week for a tour of the compound he was building in the hills of Woodside, 30 miles south of San Francisco. Six years in the making and much anticipated in architectural circles, Ellison's 23-acre complex will be what Kubla Khan would have built if he'd had a Japan fetish and a budget that could reach $100 million. It will serve the tidy purpose of outdoing Gates's $50-million home on Lake Washington, the mention of which prompts Ellison to wince as if he smelled something fetid. He quotes his friend, Apple chief executive Steve Jobs: "I don't begrudge Microsoft their success. It's just that they have no taste."

The chief designer of Ellison's project is a Zen monk; it will replicate a sixteenth-century Japanese village. Expert craftsmen are building pieces of it in Japan, disassembling them, and shipping them to California for reassembly on-site. Stones for the walls were hand-cut in the Far East ("hard to find high-quality masons here"). "It will be the most serene living environment ever built," he says. And a cultural treasure: "The most important Japanese project to be built in the last two hundred years." The president of Oracle's Japanese subsidiary cried when he saw the site, Ellison tells me.

Few people outside of Ellison's 100-person construction team have seen the compound, so the invitation was well worth a return trip to California from Washington. Two Mondays later, I received a call from Oracle PR chief Jennifer Glass. Ellison would lead the tour that Wednesday at 12:30 P.M. she said.

I booked a hasty—and expensive—flight and met Glass at 11:30 at Oracle's headquarters in Redwood Shores. We were drinking bottled water in a cafeteria when Glass's cell phone rang. It was Ellison's office. No tour today, they said. No reason given. What if I extended my trip and we did it the next day or the day after? I could do that. Sorry, they said. Larry might be going out of town. But I was free to go look at the construction site. Glass would be happy to drive me over.

We rode a half-hour on redwood-shaded and winding mountain roads. We got lost. Glass called Ellison's office for better directions. We turned around, got back on track. Then, a few minutes from the site, her cell phone rang again. Ellison's office. "Larry's on his way over. He'll see you in five minutes."

When we arrived, he was already there. He mentioned that we were late.

OUR PRIMEVAL ENVIRONMENT

"It's the ambiguity between inside and out," Ellison said as he led Glass and me on the tour of the compound. At that moment, he was pointing to a rock that is both inside and outside a shower, but he returns repeatedly to the theme of planned ambiguity.

Guests will be kept guessing. Are the trees growing out of the main residence? Is the koi pond a discrete body or connected to the three-acre lake? Is that structure over the lake a bridge or a residence? Ellison pointed to a bathroom that opens out onto the woods. "It will be like taking a bath in a redwood forest," he said.

Inside or out?

Where do you stand?

Ellison wore dark shades, white tennis shorts, and a black tank top emblazoned with the red logo of his 78-foot yacht, *Sayonara*. His thick arms were tanned, even slightly burned, and his black hair was tousled after a workout. His silver Mercedes-Benz S600 was parked in back, a hairbrush lying on the passenger seat.

He agreed to give a tour on one condition: no photographs on the grounds. He was a gracious and eloquent host, romping around the property as if leading an inspection of his idealized soul.

On a visit to Japan in the mid-1970s, Ellison said, he entered a garden and never felt more at home. The compound is intended to recreate that feeling. During my visit, it was a large construction site: Tractors zigzagged across bare dirt, half-finished structures stood draped in plastic. But some time in the next few years—Ellison was noncommittal on a completion date; it could be some time in 2002—it will comprise an 8,000-square-foot main house; five guest residences, an underground network of basements and tunnels; a forest of cherry trees; high-speed streams, low-speed streams, waterfalls, ponds, and a lake with boulders doubling as hot tubs; a tea house, boathouse, amphitheater, indoor basketball court and recreation center; a horse stable; three garages for Ellison's fourteen cars; and a sprawling garden to be maintained by a staff of twenty.

The lake will be filled with purified drinking water.

When the project is finished, Ellison will sell his $30-million, Japanese-style home in nearby Atherton. That one is modeled after the Katsura Villa in Kyoto, where the Japanese royal family once lived. He will keep his $25-million mansion in San Francisco for entertaining. He will live here with his fiancee, Melanie Craft, a 30-year-old writer (the same Melanie from that day at the Hay-Adams hotel), an Icelandic pony, the two cats named Big Daddy and Maggie, and indigenous bobcats, deer, and coyotes. His teenage son and daughter from his third marriage will have their pick of residences within the compound. He plans an influx of friends, artists, dignitaries. They will select meals with a mouse click, and food will be delivered to them by boat.

Overlooking the soon-to-be garden from a second-floor library, Ellison noted that the great Western structures—Notre Dame, Versailles—were designed to humble people before God and king. But the goal of Japanese architecture is to create a serene and familiar place. "By familiar, I mean natural," he said. "We just moved to cities a few thousand years ago. Before that, we were forest dwellers." The place is meant to integrate the most sublime creations of God and humans.

"You can smell the oils of the cedar and the pine, and that's a very reassuring smell," he said. "That's our primeval environment," in contrast to the ambience of his boyhood home in Chicago, which he distilled to "plaster and glass and gunshots."

Growing up, Ellison and his mother yearned for a house. They'd always lived in apartments. That's all they ever dreamed of, he says. When Ellison moved into his first house, in his 20s, he thought he was rich. But this compound transcends wealth, he says. It is more a life's work. By viewing this home, Ellison says, others can learn about his values, his cultural passions, his tastes. And this is important. "I am not myself an artist, but I am a patron," he said, "and I am a critic." The act of creation is what defines humankind, he says. "One of the terrible things that men have versus women is that men can't create life. We're stuck with second best."

The tour lasted two hours, inadequate for seeing the home's exquisite nuances—like speed-reading poetry," Ellison said. Every time he entered a room, workers did a double take, as if expecting a command. "You can see how it comes together like the feathers of a bird," he said pointing to a boathouse roof. Ellison held out his arms, embracing the panorama of what was to come. He smiled and laughed. "It's simply astonishing! The sensuality is incredible."

Upon his death, Ellison said he will leave the compound to Stanford University, on the condition that "they don't touch anything." Ellison is terrified of dying. He doesn't get death; it mocks his rational bent and need for control. "I don't understand how someone can be here, then not be here," he said. "It's incomprehensible." He's more terrified of getting old. A portion of his charitable giving—which overall pales in comparison to Gates's—goes to fund research at the University of California on DHEA, a hormone that some people believe could retard aging. He has also given substantial sums to cancer research.

For now, Ellison will bid for immortality with this compound. "Sometimes it bothers me," he said. "I think it will outlive Oracle."

He walks into a bathroom next to a hand-carved wooden bridge connecting two residences. He will put a bath next to the kitchen and dining areas so that guests can bathe and enjoy tea before their meals. It is a Japanese custom to bathe before meals, Ellison explained. (On a few occasions, he said, "We Japanese"). Ellison chuckled, then stared and pointed with contempt at the basin of a sink. "This wood is much too complex for me," he said. Fir and pine might work here, but not elm. Beautiful, but too grainy. "Get rid of it," he said to no one in particular.

He is a self-described "obsessive–compulsive perfectionist," and nothing will escape his full attention here. "I have driven the poor people crazy," he said, laughing. "They have suffered mightily."

At the end of the tour, Ellison led us through a series of basement rooms that would contain a state-of-the-art air-conditioning system, hot water heaters, humidifiers. "It will be a different century down here," he says. He proceeded into a long tunnel that connected a garage with the main residence. For about 30 seconds, we were in total darkness. Yet Ellison kept up his brisk walk, getting several feet ahead before calling back to us from the end of the tunnel. "When you get to where I am," he said, his voice echoing, "you can see the light." Then he laughed.

WHERE YOU STOOD

Theories abound on what caused Larry Ellison.

"I think the distant and disapproving father created a maverick son," Jenny Overstreet said. Louis Ellison gave his son "so much fuel, so much anger, perseverance, and determination," said Overstreet, who now lives in a San Francisco mansion down the street from her former boss's. "It was great for all of us."

The trauma of abandonment? "So my biological mother abandoned me, and my mother who raised me abandoned me when she died of cancer," Ellison said. "I've thought of all this. It's one of those things that just sounds so good, the reasons are all there." He took a deep and melodramatic breath.

"But is it really true?"

Starting from his birth, on August 17, 1944, Ellison's biography has been steeped in uncertainty. Errol Getner, his next-door neighbor in adolescence, says Ellison always told him that his father worked for the FBI. Over the years, Ellison has often spoken about the "projects" and the "ghetto" he grew up in. And the gunfire. "He used to tell me that the two toughest kids from his neighborhood were Cassius Clay and Sonny Liston," said Gary Kennedy, a former top executive at Oracle. The future Muhammad Ali grew up in Louisville, Liston in Arkansas and St. Louis. Both spent time in Chicago later in their lives, miles from where Ellison lived.

People from Ellison's South Side neighborhood describe a cozy, solidly middle-class and heavily Jewish enclave. There were pockets of Italians, Irish, Puerto Ricans, and African Americans nearby. Ellison encountered anti-Semitism, but it was "just one particular brand of anti," he said.

"If you took the TV shows 'Happy Days' and 'Brooklyn Bridge' and averaged them, we would be somewhere in the middle," said Chuck Weiss, a childhood friend who now works at Oracle. "We weren't quite as suburban as 'Happy Days,' not quite as urban or ethnic as 'Brooklyn Bridge.'" The neighborhood became crime- and drug-infested in the late 1960s, after Ellison had left.

Lillian and Louis Ellison lived in a two-bedroom apartment on Clyde Avenue near 82nd street, about one mile west of Lake Michigan. They lived on the top floor of what was known as a "four-flat" apartment; there was a living room in front, kitchen and dining room in back, adjoined by Larry's room, which was always a mess. Lillian was a bookkeeper, Louis an auditor for the U.S. Bureau of Indian Affairs, and they survive in their son's memory as opposites: Larry described her as a loving and committed mother, him as quiet and scornful. Louis, he said with derision, had "an automatic and unthinking deference to authority figures and rules. . . . He was a true believer." One thing he believed—or said a lot—was that his son would never amount to anything. "That was his form of greeting, as opposed to, 'Hi' or 'Good morning,'" Larry said.

Louis had a daughter from a previous marriage, Doris, who was nineteen years older than Larry. She too recalls Louis as a remote, aloof man. "I have no memory of my father ever touching me, hugging me, or of sitting on his lap," says Doris Linn. She and her husband, Chicago judge David Linn, lived next door, and they served as alternative mentors to Larry. He would bring friends over to view David's closet of fine suits. He became transfixed by any demonstration of marked intelligence. He and Doris had a favorite game they played: Ellison would open an encyclopedia to a random person, place, phenomenon; he would say what it was, and Doris would throw back a quick definition. Ellison would become enraptured by this, or any demonstration of intelligence.

Larry defied his parents' wishes that he have a bar mitzvah, signaling a lifelong indifference to Jewish customs. Hebrew school conflicted with his Little League practice. "I was a pitcher, and it was a matter of giving up pitching to learn Hebrew or not," Ellison said. "So I decided to go to baseball practice." He is glib about this now, but friends recall Ellison's refusal to have a bar mitzvah as a major act of rebellion at the time, one that heightened the already tense environment at 8237 Clyde Street.

Ellison's boyhood companions recall a child of outsized dreams. "Whatever he was doing, he was always projecting it bigger and better," said Jimmy Linn, Doris and David's son, five years younger than his uncle. Ellison, he says, was "extremely bright, but a little unbridled."

At South Shore High School, Ellison "always seemed quiet and preoccupied, not part of the in crowd," said Sheila Maydet Gutterman, the valedictorian of Ellison's Class of 1962, now a divorce lawyer in Denver. "Usually, in high school, you know where someone is coming from. But Larry always seemed to have Plexiglas around him. You could never really get a sense of who he was." Ellison was tall and awkward, with greasy olive skin and pimples, Gutterman recalls. "I don't think people were particularly nice to him."

Ellison had a reputation for making up elaborate stories, something his friends and classmates often mentioned. "Larry's ability to embellish reality was just amazing," said Dennis Coleman. Ellison's friends are somewhat sympathetic to this tendency, owing it to his ever-active imagination and his boredom with the prosaic facts of reality. He was avidly curious, and he was always reading—*Scientific American* magazine, Will and Ariel Durant's *Story of Civilization,* the Bible, biographies of Churchill, General Douglas MacArthur, books on World War II, and any newspaper article he'd see on sports greats Ernie Banks, Sandy Koufax, Mickey Mantle, Bobby Hull, or Gordie Howe.

But Ellison skipped classes, received frequent detention, and earned mixed grades. He got along poorly with most of his teachers. Today, Ellison often posits them, like his father, as ready foils for his iconoclasm. "Never do you make teachers happier than when you do exactly what they tell you to do," he said. "They just really love that. And you never can succeed in business by following the rules."

Once, Ellison's biology teacher, Mrs. Coleman, Dennis Coleman's mother, threatened to flunk him for cutting class. "If I get the highest grade on the final, would you still flunk me?" Ellison said. Yes, she said, and forty years later, he recreates their argument with a taunting edge. "If I know more about biology than anyone else in class, you're gonna flunk me?" he said, waving his hands, smirking. It is as if Mrs. Coleman, who died in 1975, were sitting next to him.

Right next to her is his Latin teacher, the miserable Latin teacher who told Ellison that if he failed Latin, it would ruin his life. "A letter in a rectangle will ruin your life? I don't think so," Ellison said, shaking his head. "I can imagine being hit by a car would ruin your life." But why would he need to learn Latin? "I was quite certain that I wouldn't become a priest." He laughed again, a quick and righteous chuckle.

Ellison had a harder time remembering when he learned that he had been adopted. He was about 12, and Louis told him in mid-conversation. Or maybe it was mid-argument. "My short-term memory was erased," Ellison said. "All the circumstances I remember about being told were just whited out. I just remember that one realization and having to deal with it."

He didn't tell his friends he had been adopted. It was simply not something he spoke about, though he spoke about most other things. Ellison was an expert at banter. "He had a knack for taking your position and turning it into a total absurdity," said boyhood friend Rick Rosenfield, who would later start the California Pizza Kitchen restaurant chain. Dennis Coleman recalled one of Ellison's oft-repeated manifestoes: "There's no such thing as pleasure. There's only tension and the release of tension."

Ellison's social life was steeped in male camaraderie. His inner circle included no females, a characteristic basically unchanged through his career in business. In college he joined a Jewish fraternity, Tau Epsilon Pi (the Tommies), which also included his closest friends—Getner, Coleman, and Rosenfield. They rode around with Ellison in his 1956 Dodge with a push-button transmission. They took forays downtown to Rush Street to try, generally unsuccessfully, to pick up girls. Ellison lifted weights, jogged before it was popular, and worked as a lifeguard for the city of Chicago. He loved the certainty of athletic competitions, especially basketball and football. "Freud defines maturity as the ability to defer gratification," Ellison said, in explaining the appeal of sports. "That's the reason sports is so popular. You let go of a ball, and half a second later, you know whether you're gratified or not. It was always very clear where you stood."

The rest was not so simple. Ellison and Errol Getner commiserated on free-floating anguish. They both describe times of isolation and despair—qualities familiar to most teenagers—and ones that seemed to bond Ellison and Getner especially. "It seemed like the only time we could forget our pain was when we were competing at something," Getner said.

Yet both men speak of their adolescent days with nostalgia. On warm summer nights, they could walk to Carl's Hot Dogs at 82nd and Jeffrey. For 25 cents, they purchased a hot dog on a steamed poppy-seed bun with kosher pickles and a bag of greasy fries. Later, they would put on $10 Converse All-Stars and take long runs through dark Chicago streets late at night. They would then walk two blocks to South Chicago Avenue, where they would purchase twelve glazed doughnuts and a half-gallon of milk. And they would talk, talk, talk all night about books, about girls, about making money.

"Your deepest friendships, and sometimes your most profound emotional experiences, occur when you're a teenager," Ellison said. "You were so emotional, and the world was just revealing itself to you. Sometimes it's beautiful and sometimes it's painful. And sometimes it's the same thing."

RECONSTRUCTION

Ellison's most profound teenage relationship was with Karen Rutzky, his girlfriend from age 15. Rutzky's parents did not like him, and "Larry was devastated by that," Doris Linn said.

But Ellison and Rutzky attended three proms and owned three matching shirts. Lillian gave her son money, and he would take Rutzky out, and buy her gifts. He gave her a Mary Poppins book. The inscription: "To Karen, a supercalifragilisticexpialidocious date and a truly tolerant person. Love always, Larry."

Their relationship continued after she left for the University of Michigan. He told her that he planned to go to medical school, and he asked her to quit school and become a secretary to support him. She refused, just as she would refuse two marriage proposals in their five years together. Ellison remembers just one proposal.

As with many relationships from his past, Ellison's memory differed starkly from the other person's. The details are long ago and unimportant. In sum: "I cared deeply about Larry," said Karen Rutzky Back, now of Los Angeles. But he lied to her serially, she said. "I got tired of being a detective about everything he said."

Ellison said the notion that he lied to her is "really breathtaking." He added: "The fact that I stayed with Karen Rutzky for five years is one of the worst things anyone can say about me," he said. "Forget about always being late." Ellison rooted against University of Michigan sports teams for twenty-five years.

In the middle of the tour of his future home, Ellison felt compelled to tell me that the best-looking girl in his high school had a crush on him. But he did not go out with her because he was loyal to Rutzky. "The single stupidest mistake I made in my entire life," he said. Over several hours of interviews, no subject animated Ellison more than Rutzky. For all his success, her rejection—and her parents' dislike—seemed a lingering embodiment of all that made him feel unworthy. It also served as a ready benchmark for his life's piece-by-piece reconstruction.

"You know, I was named one of *Playboy*'s top ten best-dressed people recently," he told me in a phone conversation in late 2000. "I think my journey from those stupid matching shirts with Karen Rutzky to *Playboy*'s best-dressed list is a more heroic journey than going from the South Side of Chicago to running Oracle."

In 1962, Ellison graduated from South Shore High School and enrolled at the University of Illinois in Urbana-Champaign. He followed the same basic scholastic method he did in high school: If a subject interested him, he worked hard; if it didn't, he didn't. One of his chief accomplishments came in an intra-fraternity "Car

Bash" competition: The broad and muscular Ellison helped his team smash the guts out of a junkermobile with a sledgehammer.

At the end of his sophomore year, Lillian Ellison died of kidney cancer. Crushed, Larry left school, returned to Chicago, and cried for weeks. He never returned to Urbana-Champaign.

In the summer of 1964, he and Chuck Weiss visited Northern California. They spent time in Berkeley, at the beginning of the counterculture movement. Ellison was not of the drug or protest realms; he registered for the draft and said he would have gone to Vietnam if called. But he "grew his hair a little long and strummed a little guitar," Jimmy Linn recalled. Ellison was captivated by California, "the promised land." It seemed wild, open, and warm, a perfect place for escaping cohabitation with Louis.

But he returned home to Chicago, where many of his friends were attending Northwestern University. He enrolled as a part-time student at the University of Chicago, where he spent one semester. He told friends that he had gotten into medical school. He even produced an acceptance letter. "The letter didn't look legit," says Dennis Coleman, then an undergraduate at Northwestern. Coleman remembered that Ellison's letter was from the University of Southern California. "It was very short and had typos." Rutzky also recalled Ellison showing her an acceptance letter.

Ellison never applied to medical school, he says now. He didn't graduate from college, or come close. What about the acceptance letter? "It just couldn't be," he said. He asserted the logical impossibility of the premise—it just "couldn't be" that there was an acceptance letter, because there was never an acceptance medical school—and ignores the charge that he ever fabricated a letter.

In the overall scheme of Larry Ellison's success, lying about a medical school acceptance is not that relevant. One can even understand his impulse to embellish credentials in the achievement-oriented worlds of Karen Rutzky, Dennis Coleman, and his other friends. But the lengths to which Ellison has perpetrated the notion of this acceptance—to this day, and to the people closest to him—is remarkable. When I spoke to Doris and Jimmy Linn, both of them still believed that Ellison had been accepted at medical school. They recalled David Linn's dismay when Ellison said he wouldn't be going to medical school: "You'll be the first man in five thousand years of the Jewish religion who was accepted to medical school but refused to go," he said.

Instead, Ellison bought himself a turquoise 1964 Thunderbird and drove west. He had no idea how he would support himself, but in an undergraduate physics class he had shown some aptitude in computer programming.

BREAKAWAY

Silicon Valley still sprawled with cherry orchards in the summer of 1966. But some early pillars of the future high-tech metropolis were in place: Stanford and the University of California at Berkeley were turning out litters of engineers, many of whom took jobs at local computer hardware makers such as Hewlett Packard and Fairchild Camera and Instrument Corp. A high proportion of Bay Area business were using mainframe computers.

Carrying a programming manual, Ellison moved from technical job to technical job at banks, insurance companies, and small businesses. He made enough money to live on, and he loved the notion that he was "amounting to something" on his own.

In 1967, he met Adda Quinn at a San Jose employment agency, and they married after a few months, both at 23. Quinn's brother was his best man, and no one from Chicago attended the wedding, except for Weiss, who was living in San Francisco. "Larry seemed to sort of drop out of sight for a while," Jimmy Linn said.

Ellison seemed determined to break clean from his past, although Quinn says he often mentioned Karen Rutzky. He got his nose fixed, smoothing out the lumps from long-ago basketball games. But he couldn't go to just any plastic surgeon; he insisted on the biggest name in Beverly Hills, Dr. Maury Parks, aka "The Nose Doctor." As she turned the pages of old photo albums, Quinn compared Ellison photos pre- and post-nose job. "Look at this," she said, pointing to the crooked and knobby nose from their wedding day, "and this," as she points to the renovated version a few years later. "I paid for that nose!"

The Ellison-Quinn household could not afford Dr. Maury Parks. Nor could they afford Larry's $1,000 racing bike or $30,000 sailboat or the $100 a month he needed to repair his car or the expensive wallpaper for the house they bought in Oakland in 1970. But Ellison insisted on all of them, and Quinn paid. Ellison kept talking about getting better-paying jobs to support his champagne tastes, but he made a series of lateral career moves, and some backward ones.

When his beloved cat, Yitzak (for Yitzak Rabin), died, Ellison was so distraught that he stayed home for a week. He always loved cats, and took death—any death—exceedingly hard. His employers had limited patience for his needs and desires. So, increasingly, did Quinn. Ellison enrolled in graduate classes at Berkeley, but would never finish. "He told me that he graduated from an obscure college in Sheffield, England," Quinn said. "Now, where do you suppose he dreamed that up."

"He told me these big, whopping lies, and he stuck to them," Quinn said. "He could follow these lies for years."

"I've never been to Sheffield, England," Ellison said. "So that's very peculiar." He said nothing about whether that's what he had led Quinn to believe.

Ellison's lack of a college degree puts him in superb company among high-tech entrepreneurs. Bill Gates and Steve Jobs didn't finish college, either. To succeed in Silicon Valley without a traditional degree is something of a credential itself—proof that a genius is above convention. But Ellison hardly wears his limited schooling as a badge of renegade credibility. Indeed, it has been a point of recurring shame in his life.

There is no better indicator of this than Ellison's refusal to tell his own wife that he did not have a bachelor's degree. They were married seven years.

Why did he never tell her? Because they met at an employment agency, Ellison explains, and he told people there he had a degree in order to get jobs. And he could never bring himself to come clean to his wife. "I lied," he said. "It's a bad thing. I'm embarrassed."

Quinn calls Ellison the most charming, brilliant, and nonboring man she has ever known. He also gave her an ulcer, she says, with his deceptions, darting interests, and changing moods. She would ask him if he paid their real estate taxes, he would say yes, and, a few days later, a delinquent notice would come in the mail. Ellison would spend large stretches of time out of the house. When he was home, he and Quinn would argue. He had an explosive temper, and Quinn said she feared for her safety as their marriage was ending. The couple kept guns in the house—they lived in a rough part of Oakland and had been burglarized—and she thought Ellison was becoming increasingly erratic.

"I don't know how she could have feared for her safety," Ellison said, and calls himself a nonviolent person. "The fact that she ever thought I could shoot her is a little bizarre."

In 1971, Ellison invited his aging father to live with him. It was a kind and unexpected gesture, Quinn says, but their strain lingered. Louis was not disapproving, she observed; she never heard him criticize his son. But neither was he supportive, and Larry took that as disapproval.

"Louis would kind of look down, with this expression," Quinn said. "It would drive Larry absolutely crazy." Louis stayed until 1974, when he entered a nursing home, and died soon afterward.

Ellison's marriage to Quinn ended the same year. He didn't want it to. He badgered her for several nights in a row, not letting her sleep, pleading with her. He, like Quinn, was unhappy in the marriage, but something about its stability appealed to him. They tried counseling. "I remember asking, how does this work?" Ellison said. "And I got this amazing gibberish answer. I'm like, okay, great, thanks. Uh, no."

"He was so smart, he could almost outguess what the psychiatrist would say," Quinn recalls. "I didn't trust him with mind games, because he's the best. And I think that's why he's so good in business."

In one counseling session, Quinn says, Ellison vowed that, if she stayed with him, he would make a million dollars. It was the first time she had heard him speak of becoming rich. "I said to him, I hope you become a millionaire," Quinn said. "Maybe that's what it will take to make you happy."

Years later, Ellison bought Quinn a $50,000 Mercedes, and he paid the mortgage on her parents' house. When Quinn's second husband battled cancer, Ellison gave him a lucrative job. He is on good terms with all three of his former wives, he said.

Despite his scattershot job history, Ellison was becoming a good computer programmer. In the mid-1970s, he landed at Ampex, a computing firm in Sunnyvale, which, like many companies in the early days of Silicon Valley, did contract work for the federal government. Ellison contributed to a database project for the CIA. Code name: Oracle.

At the time, databases were usually "hierarchical." They organized data according to a "hierarchy" of information. If Pan American Airlines wanted to keep track of its flights (What are the flight numbers? Where are they going?) the information would flow downward from a master heading marked "flights." Users would start at the top of a chart and work their way down to find the information they were looking for.

But database technology was nearing a breakthrough. In 1970, International Business Machines Corp. researcher Ted Codd published a plan for a "relational" database, which could discern fluid connections between bits of data. With a relational database, a Pan American employee could tell, say, how many passengers on Flight 209 had ordered vegetarian meals. Chrysler could see which models were selling best, and who was selling the most. Codd's paper prompted a race to create the best relational database. The key players were a group from IBM, called System R, and another from Berkeley, Ingres. In 1976, the IBM scientists completed their plan and published it. That would be unthinkable today, but in the 1970s, software was a largely academic pursuit. The satisfaction of prestige and authorship were viable currencies. There was also a utopian ideal, a virtue in sharing information because it would enrich the larger academic village. "Our feeling was, the rising tide lifts all ships," said Michael Blasgen of the IBM team. "Since IBM was the biggest ship, we stood to benefit most."

No one benefited more than Larry Ellison.

AGGRESSIVE PROMISCUITY

"We can do this," Ellison thought as he read the IBM paper. For the first time, someone had applied a mathematically consistent means of finding and retrieving data. He was amazed and impressed. Yet he wasn't thinking about the paper so much as an intellectual challenge to replicate. Foremost in Ellison's mind was that this was a business opportunity.

In 1977, at age 32, Ellison had started a software development consultancy with two former colleagues, Bob Miner and Ed

Oates. As in school, Ellison had struggled with traditional work tenets—things like being on time, keeping a boss happy.

"He never seemed to care that much about other people," said Irv Tjomsland, the manager of a software development project that Ellison worked on at Ampex in the early 1970s. "He was one of those people where, if someone else on the team had a problem, it was that person's problem. But if Ellison had a problem, it was everybody's problem."

Ellison was much better suited to being his own boss. It would allow him to operate at Larryspeed, in Larrytime. He recalled a dispute he had with a manager at Omex, a Silicon Valley firm where he worked briefly in the 1970s. He was admonished by a manager for coming in at 11 A.M.

"So, are any of my projects late?" Ellison recalled saying.

"No."

"Are anyone else's projects on time?"

"No."

"Well," Ellison said, his voice rising again at the recollection, "maybe everyone should get some extra sleep. You clearly have a decision to make."

It was around this time, 1977, that David Linn received a phone call one night. Ellison needed some money to start his own business, and Linn agreed to write him a check. "Well," Linn said as he got off the phone, "there goes $6,000."

The same year that Ellison, Oates, and Miner started their consulting firm, Bill Gates and Paul Allen started a company called Micro-soft in an apartment in Albuquerque, New Mexico. While Micro-soft would transform computing for individuals, Ellison's team focused on businesses. Their goal was to build the first commercially viable relational database. With IBM's paper as a blueprint, Ellison felt that they could develop a better product and sell it first.

Ellison did nothing to hide his reliance on the IBM team. Blasgen recalled getting a letter from Ellison: "He basically said, give me a few details, I'll copy them, and that way our systems will be the same," The request was ignored.

Ellison, Miner, and Oates had limited resources; venture capital did not flow then as it does today, and besides, Ellison had no interest in diluting his ownership in the company. They began as a bootstrap operation: sign clients, do work, get money, develop their database product. And despite their small size and limited resources, Ellison, Miner, and Oates were well-positioned to thrive in a wide-open market. Since they had written their products in IBM's SQL ("Sequel") programming language, as opposed to Ingres's QUEL language, they benefited from a 1986 decision to make SQL the industry standard. As an independent consultancy, Ellison's team could shift its strategic direction from client to client, all the while amassing funds from each contract. They worked on a range of projects. When they decided to build and patent a software product, they designed it to be "portable," meaning it would run on different computing platforms. Ellison liked to say that their software was "promiscuous."

They named the product Oracle and put the first version on the market in 1979—three years ahead of IBM. Within five years, the company that would become known as Oracle Corp. was generating $12.7-million a year in sales. On March 12, 1986, Oracle held an initial public offering. Shares debuted at $15 and closed that day at $20.75. Ellison's 34-percent stake was worth $93 million. Microsoft, which had since eliminated the hyphen from its name and held its IPO the next day, priced at $21 and closed at $28, putting Gates's stake at $300 million.

As Oracle grew, so did Ellison's craving for dominance, a notion fostered on frequent visits to the Far East. He once met a Japanese businessman, a Fujitsu executive, who mocked his American counterparts for voicing "great respect" for their rivals. "In Japan, we believe our competitors are stealing rice out of the mouths of our children," the businessman said. "We must destroy our competition."

Ellison returned to Oracle and made reference to that conversation repeatedly. He spoke of "cutting off the oxygen" of his competitors and ending his meetings with a chant of "kill, kill, kill."

While much of Oracle's success was a triumph of technical skill and raw competitiveness, it also stemmed from one of the most aggressive sales forces in computing history. The company's sales reps were pushed hard and paid well—Marc Benioff, at 25, was making $300,000 a year in 1986; top-flight sellers were making seven figures. "The management theory was simple," Benioff said. "Go out and don't come back before you have a signed contract." If sales reps missed their numbers, which usually meant doubling sales every year, they wouldn't last.

When I mentioned Oracle's vaunted "sales culture" to Ellison, he scrunched up his face. Sales, while the lifeblood of any business, carry a stigma in Silicon Valley, where innovation rules. If you succeed, you want it to be because you've built something better, not because you sold it better. "Could our sales force convince someone to buy a product that wasn't any good?" he says. "Maybe. Would they keep buying? Would they keep being influenced by a salesman's pitches over a golf game? We must have pretty good technology."

But in the late 1980s, no one else was selling harder than Ellison. The relational database market was in a land-grab period, analogous to what Internet commerce was undergoing in the late 1990s. Getting market share was everything, even if it meant slashing prices to nearly zero. It would undercut competitors—and keep sales bonuses coming in—even if it might cut into revenue later on. Several sources recall Ellison exaggerating what his software could do and when it would be ready, all in the interests of winning an account. "Ellison was perfectly willing to lie to customers," says Michael Stonebreaker, the former chief executive of Ingres, which would be Oracle's chief competitor in the 1980s.

"Were there things we promised in our early years that we couldn't do?" Ellison said. "I'm sure there were."

"Larry always said, 'I have a little problem with tenses,'" Benioff recalled. When Ellison promised a customer something, he believed it at that moment, said Gary Kennedy, who oversaw Oracle's sales operation in the late 1980s. "Larry wasn't so much dishonest as he was imprecise to gain an advantage."

Customers would become enraged. But they needed Oracle's software to make their companies more efficient; and to find a new database vendor—given the complexity involved in replacing an elaborately customized system—would be massively disruptive to a business. One of the more popular recources for frustrated customers was to sue Oracle. They did so in large numbers. (When I went to the San Mateo County Courthouse to see dockets on suits filed against Oracle, the records clerk said, "I hope you have all day.") Ellison didn't care. "That's why I have a legal staff," he would say, and it was emblematic of the company's attitude toward customers generally. "There was always e-mail floating around Oracle about how stupid various customers were," said Unang Gupta, Oracle's seventeenth employee and a longtime executive.

Ellison could be brilliant in one-on-one sales meetings with customers; he could speak the language of engineers and marketeers alike. But scheduling these meetings, and getting him to these meetings, was always a monumental challenge—to say nothing of getting him to tell the truth in these meetings. Kennedy remembers a team of executives from a major customer, Caterpillar, traveling from Peoria to San Francisco to meet with Ellison, only to have Ellison not show up. The meeting was rescheduled for a few weeks later. The executives returned to San Francisco—and Ellison didn't show up again.

During this period Ellison could be inspiring or abusive to work for. "You would spend a lot of time anticipating what Larry would do next," said Gupta. His hiring and firing patterns were unpredictable. Ellison viewed business relationships as transient, a phenomenon that extended to wives, two more of whom came and went before 1986. Whatever his beliefs and methods, he could justify them by success. Oracle was the dominant maker of database software at a time when businesses were pouring cash into information technology. He was an overnight king in Silicon Valley. But Ellison never got as much attention as the other software mogul to the north, Bill Gates.

In 1989, with more than 4,000 employees, Oracle moved to a verdant sprawl of ponds and cylindrical glass towers on U.S. 101 twenty-five miles south of San Francisco. In a valley dominated by beige office parks, the lush campus became known as "the Emerald City" (also "Larryland"), with Mercedes-Benzes, Jaguars, even Rolls-Royces lining the parking lots. Ellison, who drove a red Ferrari to work, began boasting about the hours of tennis he played on company time. He dated a procession of women, some of whom were his employees. His rare appearances at headquarters were dubbed "Elvis sightings."

The good times came at a price. "Larry Ellison has created more millionaires than anyone [else] in Silicon Valley," said Igor Sill, an executive search consultant who did work for Oracle from 1984 to 1990. "And most of them wind up hating him."

This is perhaps overstated, and it ignores the ambiguity of feeling that Ellison incites in people. Many former employees who have fallen out with him speak generously in retrospect. "The people who dislike Larry, of which they are legion, tend to underestimate his brilliance," said Gary Kennedy, who left, on bad terms, in 1990.

Ending life at Larryspeed can be disorienting. "When you're doing anything so passionately, so emotionally, ending it is hard," Jenny Overstreet said. "I left in the most positive way possible, and it took me six months to come to grips with not being there."

It's rare that relationships end in the most positive way possible when it comes to leaving Oracle. The closer the employee works with Ellison, the worse it tends to get. "Larry takes anyone leaving as a personal betrayal," said John Luongo, a longtime Oracle executive who left on good terms, but at a point where the company was about to implode from its excesses.

Ellison speaks well of Luongo, and says he did not feel betrayed when he left the company. "I felt, if anything, abandoned."

A NEAR CORPORATE DEATH

In 1990, Oracle started paying some sales commissions in gold. It would be the final indulgence of a company that seemed to be on a perpetual joyride.

Years of sales discounts, coupled with sloppy accounting methods, led Oracle to record revenues it had not received. The company reported nearly $971 million in sales in 1990—and yet had a large proportion of uncollected bills. It was forced to "restate" revenues in September 1990, and after more than a decade of doubled sales each year, Oracle posted a loss of $12.4 million in 1991. Several executives and top managers fled. Ellison fired others. The company's stock value plummeted from $3.8 billion to $700 million. In November of 1990, shares of Oracle reached their all-time low, $4.88. Ellison's stake in the company was then worth $164 million, down from nearly a billion the previous spring.

Things were so bad, Ellison says, that at one point, his chief accountant, Steve Imbler, walked into his office and said that the company would soon be unable to function as an independent entity. "Steve said, 'We could go bankrupt. We'd have to sell ourselves at an auction price.' Fortunately, he was wrong."

But for Ellison, this was by far the most difficult period of his professional life. When Oracle laid off 500 employees in 1991, he couldn't bring himself to leave his house. "I was too depressed," he said. "I let everyone down." Ellison takes any loss and any disappointment brutally hard, his friends say. One compares him with an alcoholic who can't bring himself to change until he hits bottom. "Larry is not very good about rolling up his sleeves and going back to work unless he has completely analyzed the reasons why he needs to do it," said Jenny Overstreet.

What had happened to Oracle was easy, though unpleasant, to discern: Ellison had spent most of his mental energy on technology issues, neglecting such business fundamentals as finance and day-to-day operations. After a period of soul-searching, he resolved to run Oracle like an "adult" business. This meant his renewed engagement. It also meant bringing in seasoned executives, like Ray Lane, whom he hired in 1992 from the consulting firm Booz-Allen & Hamilton to shore up Oracle's operations. Lane, and new financial chief Jeff Henley, spearheaded Oracle's return to health in 1992. The company earned $61.5 million that year, on sales of $1.2 billion. Ellison survived what he calls "my near corporate death" in the early 1990s, and a series of near-real ones as the decade wore on. He broke his neck in a body-surfing accident and endured four major operations on his left arm after a bike accident. He regularly made headlines for matters unrelated to software: An avid pilot, he battled the Bureau of Alcohol, Tobacco and Firearms to import a Soviet MiG-29; thwarted, he settled for an Italian jetfighter, a Marchetti. He appeared on "Oprah" and made a public plea for a wife.

He tried to become a more respectful leader. There was no specific incident or revelation, he said, although the financial crisis left him humbled. It was something that just came with age and, his friends say, loneliness. He also became increasingly sensitive about being disliked by so many people who had worked for him—something that he had taken some perverse pleasure in during Oracle's outlaw days in the 1980s. When I was visiting him in his office, Ellison recalled a conversation he had with his sister,

Doris. He was sitting in his old bedroom on Clyde Street when she walked in and posed a question.

"What's more important to you, to be admired or to be loved?" she asked him.

"That's easy, to be admired," he said.

"Wrong."

"Doris, you said what's more important to ME, and I answered."

"Yes, Larry, you did, and I told you that you were wrong."

"Get out of my room."

She left.

Ellison was contemplating this exchange forty-five years later. His sister was right, he said now. And he's been taking stock of his past behavior. "I used to practice what I jokingly referred to as 'management by ridicule,'" he said. "People would be terrified to come into meetings." Ellison vowed to be more gracious, which coincided with another turning point in his life. After years of curiosity, he hired a private investigator to locate his biological mother, Florence Spellman of New Haven, Connecticut. He called her; they spoke briefly. She had no idea what her son had become. Ellison bought her a house in California. "Bringing her out here and having her be proud of him was one of the real watersheds in Larry's life," Adda Quinn said. Ellison paid Spellman's daughter's college tuition. They kept in contact until she died in 1999.

Ellison said he absolutely forgave Spellman for giving him up for adoption. "She was very young herself and she wasn't married," Ellison said. She tried to take care of him when he was an infant, he said, but it was too difficult.

We were sitting in his office, and Ellison was smiling, and the PR woman was nodding sympathetically again, and the situation reflected nothing but warmly on Larry Ellison. Then, he couldn't resist spinning the moment. "I'm just grateful she didn't have an abortion," he said grinning.

LOOK WHAT I DID

Ellison's reunion with Florence Spellman led to another revelation. "It was very clear after meeting my real mother that she wasn't my real mother," he says. "My real mother was the woman who raised me, my real family were the people who raised me. . . . I felt completion in that I knew exactly who my family was."

Each year, Ellison invites Doris and Jimmy Linn for summer and winter cruises on the Mediterranean and in the Caribbean. He flies them to California to attend his annual party to mark the blooming of the cherry blossoms at his Atherton estate. Neither ever flies commercial. On a whim, Ellison once sent Doris a check for $5,000 to pay for damage he'd done to a black Oldsmobile she drove many decades before. In the years before he died, in 1996, David Linn rode to his judge's chambers in an Ellison-sponsored limousine. He helped fund a dot-com venture that Errol Getner had started (and later ended) in Arizona.

"Everything that Larry has accomplished has had two psychic purposes," said one longtime friend. "To say thank you to people who believed in him. And to say [expletive] you to the people who didn't."

Ellison said one of the reasons he kept his distance from childhood friends and relatives when he first arrived in California was that he wanted to succeed first. "I wanted to be able to call people and say, 'look what I did,'" he says. Today, Ellison keeps in touch with many of his old pals from Chicago. They sometimes join him on one of his yachts, where they replicate old banter and competitions. They play basketball at the hoop on board, just like on the South Side of Chicago, except that sometimes a ball bounces overboard and a deckhand will have to retrieve it with a net. There are cutthroat games of poker, with dollar antes, but if a pot gets too big, Ellison, a horrible bluffer, will declare it too rich for his blood and fold his hand. Rick Rosenfield remembers

Ellison saying this one summer as they were cruising from Capri to Sardinia at about 1 A.M. It occurred to him then that the boat was probably burning between $50 to $100 of fuel per minute.

At times, Ellison seemed to get emotional when he spoke about his life. His voice softened, almost quavered as he talked about his children. "My son is six-foot two, good-looking, smart, on the basketball team. My daughter is probably the best young equestrian in the country. But I don't care about all that. They are unbelievably nice people. They are just genuinely nice people. Which is the most important thing in life."

As he said this, there was a point when I started wondering whether Ellison was serious—whether he was just dabbling in some softer version of himself, not just for my benefit, or even for the benefit of his portrayal, but for the purposes of some kind of Larrycentric game. Or maybe he was being completely sincere, and I was overly spooked by Ellison's fondness for planned ambiguity. It recalled what an Oracle manager said to me, that the company runs on Ellison's characteristic rhythms and bents. One day, Ellison will be the warmest, most caring and charming boss in the world; the next day, for no apparent reason, he will stop talking to you.

Where do you stand? Inside or out? The perpetual questions infuse Oracle's culture with a primal insecurity that mirrors that of Larry Ellison's.

THE ONE CONSTANT

From Oracle's beginnings, Ellison has always drifted in and out of its day-to-day decision-making and strategic planning. His level of engagement depended on "Larry factors"—how interested he happened to be in what Oracle was building and selling at a given time, or what else in his life he had going on. Oracle executives can go year-by-year, from 1980 till now, and point to "Larry Years" (years he was engaged), and "non-Larry Years" (years he was not): 1987–1989 were non-Larry Years; 1990–1992 were Larry Years, when he focused on saving the company from its financial ruin. After Lane and Henley were installed in 1992, Ellison backed away.

But Ellison again racheted up his Oracle activities to greet the popular arrival of the Internet in the mid-1990s. Nothing held greater potential for Oracle's corporate legend than the Internet. Before there was an information age, Oracle dealt in managing information, and as companies produced oceans of data—whether it was Amazon tracking its customers or Ford processing bids from suppliers—Oracle had never been more central to how business gets done. The company owned a lock on the database software market, with more than double the market share of its closest competitor, IBM.

But Ellison wanted more than just a stranglehold on a single, lucrative sector. He wanted omnipresence. He wanted mainstream audiences to understand what he had done and what he had built. It always irritated him that relatively few people ever touched an Oracle product. He would walk around with Steve Jobs, and people would bombard his friend with love and praise for their cherished Macs. They could envision his work, in all its candy-like colors. Ellison? Maybe they knew him as a rich guy, or as happy shareholders themselves. But his software was the domain of back-office types. "Steve sometimes accuses me of having hardware envy," Ellison says. His software, he would often say, "is the software that runs the world." But it was still a niche, and Ellison always gets bored in a restricted place. When the Internet came, the niche blew wide open with potential. The Internet offered Ellison a chance to subvert Louis Ellison's prediction for his son in the most extreme way.

"Larry told me once, 'Yes, [Oracle] missed on PCs, but the Internet is going to change all that," said Unang Gupta. It has. Computing has been decentralized. Data has never been more pervasive. Neither has Ellison at Oracle.

"It's total immersion for Larry," Steve Jobs told me, something people close to Ellison say repeatedly. (One former Oracle executive said he planned to sell his company stock when Ellison's Woodside compound was near completion because the CEO would be spending all of his time micro-managing its finishing touches.) He has overseen the development of new software products that are transforming Oracle from a pure database company to a provider of "software services." The centerpiece is an "e-business suite," a single product that Oracle sells to businesses that allows them to manage all data-related operations online.

Friends say that Ellison's full-on commitment to Oracle stems from another difficult reality: the fleeting nature of so many things in his life. He has always considered his inability to stay married to be a crushing personal failure. His terror of death and his pain over broken bonds speaks to how untenable it is for Ellison to lack control. So much in Larryland—his interests, his friendships, and his fortunes—has been so volatile. But Oracle has been the one constant. For twenty-four years, it has been his, to steer, to build in his image. The stock might fluctuate, the economy might falter, but Oracle won't be going anywhere, and Ellison won't be either.

"AHHH, WELL"

He almost was gone in 1998. Another near-death experience, this time at sea. Ellison led his 78-foot craft *Sayonara* to victory in the famed Sydney-to-Hobart yacht race, but his victory was incidental to the hurricane that swept in unexpectedly during the race, killing six sailors in the race. Ellison recalled the morning after the storm, as *Sayonara* sailed up the Derwent River, on the way to Hobart. There was an extraordinary sunrise. "The sky was amber, a prescient blue, yellow, and green," he said. The boat was greeted by the somber sound of bagpipes playing. "It was absolutely silent on the boat. We were tacking back and forth, and everyone was looking at the sky and just marveling at being alive."

In *The Proving Ground,* G. Bruce Knecht's book on the Sydney-to-Hobart race, Ellison explained why he loves to race. "There are two aspects of speed," he says. "One is the absolute notion of speed. Then there's the relative notion—trying to go faster than the next guy. I think it's the latter that is much more interesting." He said 1998 would be his last Sydney-to-Hobart race ("This is supposed to be fun. You're not supposed to die doing it."), but Ellison's life remains a perpetual quest to prove and assert his speed in the world. It goes beyond the pedestrian notions of "competing" in business, or even being an adrenaline junkie. There seems some deep psychic imperative to this for Ellison. He speaks of "winning" and "losing" interchangeably with terms such as "success" and "failure." And when he speaks of failing, he betrays a kind of soulful fear, as if winning were a form of immortality. Failing gets harder with age, he said. He was more resilient when he was younger. Now, he feels he's running out of time. "There are only so many at-bats you get." So he's leaving less to chance, delegating much less than ever in his office.

In June 2000, Ellison's hands-on fervor claimed a predictable casualty: Ray Lane. With the exception of Microsoft's Steve Ballmer and America Online's Bob Pittman, there was no high-tech deputy who had a better reputation or a higher profile in the 1990s than Lane did. He was mentioned for an array of CEO jobs; Ellison always managed to keep him at Oracle by heaping onto his already fat package of stock options.

But Lane's great reputation became increasingly irksome to Ellison, friends said, especially given Ellison's checkered one. Ellison hated the perception that Lane—not he—had turned Oracle around in the early 1990s, and that Lane was the one who was running Oracle while Ellison did the nonsoftware-related things that get written about everywhere but the business section. "It's a classic Rodney Dangerfield thing," Lane told me a few weeks after he left Oracle and went to work at the Silicon Valley Venture Capital firm Kleiner-Perkins. "Larry doesn't feel like he gets any respect. But he wants to be the guy who's seen to be driving the industry."

Tensions over credit are hardly unique in the corporate world, especially in cases that involve a powerful deputy and a CEO who does not lack for ego. Such cases are generally not hard to resolve with grace: The deputy leaves, usually for a CEO's job somewhere else; the CEO issues an effusive public thanks and sends him on his way with a vault-full of stock options.

But the Ellison–Lane parting was classic Oracle—that's to say, strained and public. Ellison froze Lane out of meetings, according to sources close to Lane. He made big decisions without consulting Lane. It was clear to anyone inside the company that Lane was on the outs, but Ellison said nothing to him. For as tenacious as Ellison is, he does not like confrontations. He resists them for as long as possible. He lets resentment build until the situation combusts.

Lane saw it coming. He initiated two conversations with Ellison—one in March of 2000 and one in May—in which he asked his boss if he wanted him to leave. Both times, Ellison said no, Lane said. Then the problem only got worse. Lane started getting much of his information about Oracle from the press. In the end, he had no meaningful responsibility left. Ellison asked him to resign, and he obliged.

Shortly after Lane's departure, both he and Ellison took part in a petulant debate about their break-up in the pages of the *Wall Street Journal*. It was terrible PR, but that's life in Larryland, where so much gentlemanly pretense is filtered out. Ellison also saw to it that Lane left Oracle a few days before $70 million in stock options would have vested. When I played dumb and asked Ellison if Lane left on good terms, he just smiled and said, "Ahhh, well. . . ."

Lane ascribed his acrimonious end at Oracle in part to "Larry being Larry." And he will certainly not be the last Oracle executive to leave on bad terms with Ellison.

But what was unique about his departure is that it was not a personality clash per se. It was simply a time in Oracle's evolution, at the so-called dawn of the Internet Age, where Ellison saw a wave coming that was too big to share. "Larry wants to be seen as the guy who built the most valuable company in the world," Lane said. "This was his chance to go down in history."

This was his chance to beat Bill Gates.

VERY PECULIAR

I was with Ellison in his office in October 2000, a few weeks after *Forbes* published its annual rankings of personal wealth. Ellison was listed at number two, behind Gates, and it galled him. He was skeptical of the rankings and smelled a conspiracy.

"*Forbes* spots Bill as many billions as he needs," Ellison said, sighing, resigned to the injustice.

Yes, this was important.

At one point I misspoke and referred to Ellison as the presumptive "Richest Man in the United States," and Ellison promptly corrected me.

"It's not just the wealthiest guy in the United States. It's the world, the planet." He paused to weigh the notion, as if it had never occurred to him before. "I'm the wealthiest guy on the planet," he said again. "That's very peculiar." He added that of course this paled in importance next to Oracle beating Microsoft, "the biggest race of all."

Even in this phase of full Oracle immersion, Ellison's world was running wholly on Larrytime. He worked at home starting at

7 in the morning, went to his gym at 10:30, returned home for lunch. He got to his office around 1 P.M. and is usually gone by 7.

At 7:30 on a Wednesday night, after a three-hour interview that included quick-hit visits to Freud, Gates, God, and Ernie Banks, Ellison stood and walked out his office door empty-handed. He carried no briefcase, no laptop, no papers. He did not check e-mail or voice mail, or consult with any of his secretaries—all of whom had left anyway. He just finished speaking, then got up to leave.

As he strode out the door, Ellison's long visage loomed over Silicon Valley through a panorama of tall windows on the eleventh floor: San Francisco was covered in fog to the north; a clean orange sun set over the Bay to the south; red headlights flashed up and down Highway 101 to the west. Ellison seemed morning-fresh in the elevator, discoursing on his sweet Chicago Bulls and the basketball court on his yacht. The next day, Oracle would announce that its profits from the last quarter had more than doubled from the same period a year before—to $501 million, beating Wall Street's expectations—and the ensuing stock jump would again briefly make Larry Ellison the richest man in the world, the planet.

He walked slowly through the darkened lobby past a big stainless steel door that looks as if it belonged on a safe. Everyone had left the building, and Ellison was home alone except for a single mysterious man—presumably a security guard of some kind—who did not speak and trailed three feet behind.

Ellison walked out the door and began to disappear into the dark and empty parking lot. But suddenly he pivoted and looked intently back at the building. Was he looking at me? Something in the lobby? The building itself? It then became apparent as he brushed his hair with his hand: Ellison was gazing back into Oracle's emerald glass, at the reflection of himself.

CHAPTER TWO

JEFF BEZOS

Everyman, Every Man for Himself

How many gas stations are there in the United States?

Jeff Bezos likes to put this question to executives who want to work at Amazon.com. It has nothing to do with Amazon's business—petroleum products are among the few things the online retailer does not sell—but everything to do with Bezos's assessment of raw intelligence. Bezos does not care about the exact number of gas stations, only the back-of-the-envelope calculation that the candidate devises: The process yields a snapshot of how the prospect's brain is wired.

While all corporate chiefs want to hire bright people, Amazon's founder prizes "genius" as a gold standard, to a sometimes unforgiving degree. Amazon's screening process occasionally includes asking younger job candidates for their SAT scores.

Bezos's appreciation for powerful minds was fostered in a series of privileged environments—in magnet programs for gifted elementary school students, at Princeton, at one of Wall Street's elite hedge funds. He was 30 years old when he founded what would become the dominant online retailer. As the era of dot-com indulgence ended, as skepticism mounted about Amazon's prospects, Bezos remained resolutely confident. He was, after all, invested in brilliance.

The philosophies Bezos applied at Amazon follow a principle he has long embraced: Intrinsic ability rules, trumping acquired skills and accumulated experience. One of Bezos's former Wall

Street co-workers dubs him "a Master of the Universe for the Internet Age," meaning he has the same blue-chip credentials and sense of invincibility that marked Wall Street in the 1980s. Bezos's designs and intentions seem to argue against the idea that Internet commerce is a newly leveled field where anyone can play because the costs of participation are so low.

Bezos spends much of his time recruiting and screening executives. One of his standard interviewing techniques is to pop oddball questions, a common practice in high-tech companies. Bezos's favorite is the one about how many gas stations there are in the United States. He asks it sheepishly, often apologizing. "I realize it's a little weird to ask things like this to people who have 800 people reporting to them somewhere," he said in an interview I conducted with him in June 2000. If the question were put to him, Bezos would draw on his own experience: He'd figure there were 3,000 people in Cotulla, Texas, where he spent his boyhood summers with his grandfather. Cotulla had two gas stations. "I'm going to say there's a gas station for every 1,500 people," he said. "And now I know there are 280 million people in the U.S. Divide that by 1,500, and there's my guess."

That figure is 186,666. The American Petroleum Institute said there are 175,000. Off the back of his envelope, Bezos came within 6.7 percent.

JEFF THINGS

In the shorthand mythology of the Internet, the Bezos story goes like this: He invented Amazon.com during a cross-country trip in a borrowed Chevy Blazer. While his wife drove, he tapped out a business plan on a laptop. He envisioned a small, profitable online bookstore. As Amazon.com soared and Bezos's paper wealth shot into the billions, he cultivated the persona of an Everyman for

Giddy Times. He spoke of his company's fortunes with the awestruck enthusiasm of a lottery winner.

This was just a happy accident, he said. The way a random snowball doesn't set out to be an avalanche—but sometimes just ends up as one—and a static landscape gets buried. No, Bezos didn't aim to build a retail empire in 1994, any more than he set out to be valedictorian of Miami's Palmetto High School Class of 1982. But as soon as he saw what outsized goals the Internet would allow for and what its investors would fund, his achiever's addiction kicked in. He couldn't help himself. "Get Big Fast" became his corporate mantra. Buoyed by a geyser of stock gains—and sustained by a heap of debt—Amazon's virtual bookshelves swelled with compact disks, videos, shaving cream, Legos, lawn furniture, and dinosaur fossils.

He couldn't just sell books. Bezos needed to overhaul commerce to turn computer screens into the new store windows. Stores would survive only if they provided something that could not be replicated online—physical ambience, beauty, entertainment value. He was not hostile to traditional retailers, only to their mediocrity. Strip malls, he would say, would not survive his uprising.

But Bezos hates the notion that he's on a crusade; he much prefers the explanation of a company founded on a road trip. As if anyone could do this, and Amazon were some fluke of the times. Bezos carries a tiny Elph camera with him everywhere, snapping photos to chronicle his joyride, in case it ends tomorrow. How did this all happen? "We were hoping to build a small, profitable company," he said at the time. "And of course, what we've done is build a large, unprofitable company." Then he would boom forth with his trademark laugh, a bray so startling that his younger siblings used to refuse to sit with him in movie theaters. It comes with a resounding hiccup in which Bezos strings six articulated "hahs" together—hah-hah-hah-hah-hah-hah!—"like a jackass gargling bumblebees," says one friend.

When I first met Jeff Bezos, in Washington in early 1999, the person I was with, upon hearing him laugh, wondered if Bezos was "disturbed." He vowed to sell his Amazon stock that day. If he did, he would have been sorry, at least in the short-term. By year's end, Amazon was the Internet's highest flyer. All the while, the Bezos laugh became the background Muzak to a dot-com exuberance that may or may not have been rational. He was named *Time* Magazine's Person of the Year for 1999, the personification of a time when possibility seemed so limitless.

It was not limitless. By June 2000, when I next saw Bezos, the company had come to embody all that was precarious (if not still possible) in Internet business. Amazon was in the midst of a brutal run of tough projections, executive defections, and stock deflation. I visited Bezos at Amazon's headquarters, a stately, twelve-story converted hospital southeast of downtown Seattle. It had all the democratic trappings of a typical dot-com: casual dress, a foosball table in the reception area, and requisite toys placed prominently on desks to underscore how nutty and young-at-heart the corporation surely was.

In the lobby was a framed certificate to mark Amazon's $1.25-billion debt offering, declaring it "The Largest Convertible Debt Offering in History." This baffled me. Not just that a document like this—proof of massive corporate arrears—would be displayed at all, but that someone at Amazon decided to display it so prominently. Still, it was a great token of a time when massive debt became something to celebrate, a testament to corporate chutzpah, to the conceit that a wild idea like Amazon was being sanctioned by a solemn Wall Street institution, in this case, Morgan Stanley.

After a security guard escorted me to the bathroom, I waited for Bezos with an Amazon PR woman in a small cafeteria off the lobby floor. We stood next to a fully assembled dinosaur fossil that Bezos purchased at an Amazon auction. "Please don't feed the Cave Bear," a sign on the fossil said. The words on the sign flowed from a photo of Bezos.

Bezos's laugh preceded his arrival. "Ah-hah-hah-HAH-HAH-HAH" rollicked down a hallway, growing louder as he moved closer. "Hi, Jeff Bezos," he said, between sips of a cup of Starbucks coffee, his fourth of the day in mid-afternoon. He wore a blue dress shirt and khakis, the everyday Bezos uniform. We walked the grounds seeking a place to sit, and Bezos offered good-natured acknowledgment—"Nice hat"—to everyone he passed, including one employee who wore no shirt. He eagerly flashed his badge at security checkpoints, as if showing his normal-guy credentials. You'd never know he was *Time*'s Person of the Year, except that the framed cover of the issue was displayed prominently in the main reception area.

No brooding nerd, Bezos is a rare extrovert among high-tech pioneers. He is 5 feet 8 and 170 pounds, but he seems endearingly smaller than life. At one point during our meeting, he spoke unabashedly, though apologetically, around a mouthful of peanut butter crackers. He fumbled with his cell phone when his wife, MacKenzie, called to remind him to bring something home ("I will. . . . Love you, too"). At 36, Bezos had thinning brown hair and puppy brown eyes that invited a mothering impulse. Several of the seventy people I interviewed about Bezos said they felt very "protective of Jeff."

Encounters with Bezos, or discussions about him, often include descriptions of "Jeff Things." It's not clear whether "Jeff Things" is an agreed-upon term of art among Bezos fans. But his brother, a former girlfriend, and several friends all invoked "Jeff Things" (or "things") to describe some kind of Bezos behavior. Or something that had happened to him. Or something that they've just deemed a Jeff Thing because its perfect absurdity so captured his aura and ethos. Like the Jeff Thing in 1997, when Bezos and his father and brother cased and stormed a 7-11 store in Florida pretending to be

Navy Seals. (They each carried walkie-talkies; Jeff's mom waited in the car.) Or when, to celebrate his 35th birthday, he planned an elaborate scavenger hunt for his closest friends in the Metropolitan Museum of Art. Or the pocket-size tool kit he started carrying everywhere after the World Trade Center was bombed in 1993. He purchased a "World Trade Center Escape Kit" for every member of his family. (This, obviously, was well before the World Trade Center was destroyed by terrorist attacks in September, 2001.)

Certain Jeff Things exist within mundane conversations. Such as the asides that wend into his discourses. They are tangential to the conversation, but they are not parenthetical asides. That implies an idea delivered as an afterthought—and Bezos speaks at a volume, and with a buoyancy, that makes nothing sound like an afterthought.

In the middle of an explanation he was giving about his elementary school days, Bezos got going on how it's always easier to shave with a cold razor and a hot face than the opposite. It's not clear how this topic came up. But, for the record, metal shrinks when it's cold, he explained, his voice rising. It makes the razor sharper. And when your face is hot, your pores open wider. This is more conducive to good shaving. He pantomimes a shaving motion with his hand, dragging two knuckles up and down his right cheek. "A cold razor after a hot shower, that's your best bet," Bezos said. "You want any other body care tips, you come to me, hah-hah-hah-hah-hah-hah." He then said he needed a bathroom break.

Another Jeff Thing: There was this one drunken evening in the south of France. Bezos and his pal Tom Karzes wandered away from a wedding reception and came upon an abandoned hotel on a hill. "It was wild and overgrown with wisteria and it didn't look safe," said Karzes, who used to work with Bezos at the Wall Street hedge fund D.E. Shaw. "Part of the enjoyment of this for Jeff was that it was precarious." Bezos found a way inside the abandoned hotel and insisted that they explore. It was like a dark maze, but

Bezos managed to lead them up to a flat roof. A tiny victory, and an object lesson in the code of Bezos: You must live in a way that will allow no regret. "Most regrets in life are of omissions, not commissions," Bezos said.

Make it memorable. And goofy. "Goofy" is the word people use most often to describe a Jeff Thing. But it's not quite goofiness. There's also an element of obsessiveness, stubborness, riskiness, randomness, and imagination to things Jeff. There's no single word for it, or combination of words. Bezos is one of those people whose being creates his own weather system. Like a mountain, or a lake, or the Amazon. You could probably say that all people, in their own way, create a force around their personality. But the Jeff Force—an attendant phenomenon to Jeff Things—is more powerful, more far-reaching, and more easily distilled than most.

Plus, it disrupted the world—massively.

A STAIRSTEP OF ACHIEVEMENT

Amazon.com is the corporate embodiment of a Jeff Thing. The company was a wild idea, taken to an extreme that imposed itself rampantly on its chosen ecosystem—in this case, the retail world and stock market. Bezos was indulged by all the necessary support networks he needed to succeed: by investors, his family, his friends. The company became both a Bezos laboratory and playground. It is also built on a kind of macro Jeff Thing: achievement.

Nearly all Jeff Things involve some hellbent pursuit of achievement, even at its most routine, day-to-day level. When Amazon moved into its current headquarters, Bezos vowed never to take the elevator to his fifth-floor office. He'll adhere to this vow even when he's sleep-deprived, jet-lagged, late for a meeting. "Now it's like a winning streak," Bezos says. "If I'm sick with the flu, I would still take ten minutes to walk up to my office rather than throw it all away. It's like, if you have perfect attendance in high school, you don't want to blow it after a while."

"Jeff's goals depend on a stairstep of achievement," said Charles Ardai, the chief executive of Juno Online Services who worked with Bezos in the early 1990s at D.E. Shaw. "It's like when you're a little kid and you're blowing bubbles. If you have a little more air left in your lungs, you want to see how far you can go with it."

Jeff Things tend to be packed in a little kid's imagery. School metaphors, playground games. The laugh, the curiosity, the excitement. They define the Bezos brand, make him one of the New Economy's most infectious figures. Is it genuine, or the handiwork of loyal friends and the Amazon image machine? I'd venture both.

But it's also easy to mistake Bezos's ebullient, accessible persona for egalitarianism, just as it's easy to mistake Amazon's mass-market appeal for a populist streak in its founder. Bezos's reality is steeped in the blue-chip performers he has always played with. To exist in the Jeff Force is to experience the paradox of lovable elitism. It helps to be brilliant.

To work with the Jeff Force, it's a requirement.

Bezos works maniacally to enforce the strictest admissions standards in corporate America. In rewriting the rules of industry, he has nurtured a culture that can be strikingly akin to a traditional high school. It is a place in which the superachievers rule, slackers are sent home, and middlers are kept back, usually in distribution warehouses and call centers.

"SO"

"There's nothing wrong with asking for SAT scores," Bezos says. Several of his employees blew away his 1450, in fact. SATs are one minor metric in Bezos's elaborate assessment of job candidates.

Bezos declares them "a terrible data point, very noisy." But the degree to which adults talk about their SATs at Amazon is extraordinary. Employees there seem to have easier recall of their scores than you'd expect. They also seem to know how their long-ago scores compare with their colleagues'. At one point in an interview, Bezos turned to his personal PR woman, Lizzie Allen, and mentioned with wonderment that some Amazon employee named Allison had scored "at least 1550" on her SATs.

During a three-hour conversation in June 2000, Bezos proclaimed nine people as "brilliant" or "a total genius." In mid-interview, an Amazon engineer named HB walked up to Bezos, who was sitting at a picnic table in a courtyard, and mock complained that he could hear Bezos laughing from his office on the eighth floor. "HB is one of our resident geniuses," Bezos said by way of introduction. HB is "an A student," the kind who sets the standard for the rest of the class.

"If you start out with A's, you get to keep A's," Bezos said. "If you start hiring B's, B's hire B's."

Is there a place for the B student at Amazon.com? "Certainly the answer is yes," said David Risher, an Amazon senior vice president. "But at the leadership level, the answer is no, in part because that person would stick out like a sore thumb, and frankly would not interact very well with Jeff."

In 1996 Bezos interviewed Joy Covey, a candidate to be Amazon's chief financial officer. He noted that she had finished second in a field of 27,000 the year she took her CPA exam. "Why not first?" Bezos asked, half kidding. Covey, who had law and business degrees from Harvard University, said she didn't study. She got the job, and remained at Amazon until early 2000.

Candidates for top Amazon positions are subjected to arduous, Socratic tests. If someone is interviewing for a high-level marketing job, Risher said, Bezos might fill a whiteboard with thirty marketing techniques and then instruct the candidate to "force rank" the techniques from top to bottom for a designated marketing initiative. "He would say, 'What would you do first, what would you do second, what would you do third?" said Risher. That would provide a close-up, real-time look at the candidate's instincts, discipline, and focus.

Senior managers are also subject to five to ten reference checks, which Bezos often conducts himself. They can take 60 minutes each and include a battery of twenty-three questions, including: Can you think of a problem that everyone thought was unsolvable that this person solved?

"If this person were really brilliant, you can remember these things," Bezos said. "If they can't think of anything, it doesn't mean they're not brilliant. But it's certainly a negative indicator."

Since superachievers often cluster, Amazon, like many high-tech firms, tends to recruit managers from a New Economy iteration of the old boys' network. Many of them graduated from the same schools and worked together at the same companies. Program manager Jonathan Leblang graduated from Palmetto High in Miami with Bezos in 1982 (Leblang ranked seventh in the class). Risher attended Princeton with Bezos and was a member of the same eating club, where, he recalls, Bezos was a ferocious player of beer pong. Risher, like several Amazon managers, came from Microsoft Corp., a company Bezos studied closely and admired for its rigorous hiring practices.

Like many technology leaders, Amazon executives trumpet their organization as a top-caliber meritocracy, an institution where skill, commitment, and drive matter most. Bezos says that brilliance alone is not all he cares about, and that Amazon's hiring process is not one-dimensional.

One of the quirks of Bezos and his Amazon team is that they always seem to start their answers with the word "So." They don't pause or say "Well," or "Umm." But, when I asked what it's like to come to work at Amazon, one manager said, "So Amazon is a dynamic environment," and when I asked Risher how Bezos expresses anger, he said, "So he tends to be melodramatic, he might put his head down on the desk and say, `If I hear that idea again, I'm gonna have to kill myself.'" The "so's" imply the instant certainty of their positions. The answer you're about to hear is simply so.

"So" is also used to veer a question to opposing logic. When I asked Bezos about the apparent lack of racial and gender diversity at Amazon, he said: "So I totally disagree with the premise of your question," and he jumped into a defense of the Amazon staff's diverse interests, sexual orientations, hometowns, and job histories. Even as its top executives and board of directors are predominantly male and white (a profile common among technology firms), Bezos's idea of diversity tends to focus on "the diversity of genius." He is committed to assembling a collection of stellar minds that are variously wired. Amazon does not provide a demographic breakdown of its employees.

"There is no Amazon.com 'type,'" it says on the "our culture" page on the Web site. "There are Amazon.com employees who have three master's degrees and speak five languages . . . people who have worked at Procter & Gamble and Microsoft . . . a professional figure skater . . . a Rhodes scholar." One of his employees was a National Spelling Bee champion, Bezos says. "You can shout out 'onomatopoeia' in the hallway, and you'll get an answer." He is looking for "a superstar dimension" in every job candidate, he said.

If there is a recurring criticism of Bezos among people who know him, and who have worked for him, it is that he can be impatient with frailty. This became increasingly difficult as Amazon grew into an organization with thousands of frontline employees—not all of whom, inevitably, were brilliant. They often worked 55 or 60 hours a week for $11 to $14 an hour, with small grants of stock options that have lost value as Amazon's stock price has declined. The employees' output and performance are monitored closely. The company has struggled with low morale and high turnover among some customer service and distribution center workers. A union-organizing campaign, uncommon at Internet companies, sprouted.

"I found the culture at Amazon to be terribly unforgiving," says Julie Drebin, who worked as an Amazon customer-service representative for two years until she left in May 2000. "If you dared to raise issues about the company, it was as if you were defying these people who were so elite, they were beyond being questioned." When I read this quote to Bezos, he did not respond. This tension goes to the crux of conflict between the Bezos persona and the Bezos value system.

Everyman, or every man for himself?

"Bezos has obviously worked hard to construct himself as this easygoing guy and accidental capitalist," said Gretchen Wilson, who has helped organize a union campaign with a group of Amazon customer-service employees for the Washington Alliance for Technology Workers. "But if you look closely at the world he is creating, it's this incredibly harsh and uptight place based on these weird, traditional notions of who is worthy."

"I love Jeff Bezos," adds a former colleague who worked with him in the early 1990s at D.E. Shaw. "But he has blind spots to certain realities, especially when it involves the limitations of other people."

Bezos himself has always inspired enormous faith—from parents, bosses, and financial backers—and the experience has nurtured in him an unusual sense of possibility. His rise has come in a series of intellectual wonderlands where he has had to contend with few limitations.

MINI-ADVENTURES

One day when Jeff was 6, he was playing with a friend and mentioned that he had attended his parents' wedding. That's impossible, the friend said. You weren't born yet. When he got home, Jeff had a question for his mother. "I explained it all to him in terms that made me comfortable," says Jackie Bezos, "which meant I was maybe dancing around the subject." What she explained was that she had been married before, it didn't work out, and she and Jeff went back to live with Nanny and Pop. Jeff looked up and quietly asked, "You mean you got a divorce?" His mother nodded.

In 1964, two weeks after she turned 17, Jackie Gise Jorgensen gave birth to a baby boy. She was a high school student in New Mexico. Eighteen months later, her marriage ended. She and her son moved back home with her parents.

"From the minute I knew Jeff was going to be born, all I wanted to do was be a good mother," says Jackie. She hauled Jeffrey to her community college classes, changing his diapers at lunchtime. He was a wondrous-eyed boy with huge ears and bright blonde hair.

When Jeff was 2, Jackie took a job as a bookkeeper at the Bank of New Mexico. There, she met Miguel Bezos, a recent immigrant from Cuba who had fled a few months before the Cuban missile crisis in 1962. He came to Miami at 16 as part of Operation Pedro Pan, a relief program devised by a Catholic priest to bring teenagers to the United States and out of Castro's Cuba. Miguel and a cousin moved briefly to Delaware to finish high school. Then o Washington D.C. where he held several jobs, including working at McDonald's. Miguel ultimately moved to New Mexico, where the University of Albuquerque was offering scholarships to Cuban refugees. He took a part-time job at the bank of New Mexico.

Miguel says he fell in love with Jackie at the same time he did with her son. With his Cuban accent, he pronounced their names "Yackie" and "Yeff." He and Jackie married when Jeff was 4, and Miguel legally adopted Jeff, who'd already been calling him "Daddy."

When Jeff was 5 and 6, his siblings, Christina and Mark, were born. Miguel took a job as an engineer at Exxon Corp. in Houston, working long hours. "He is the least lazy person I know," Jeff said of Miguel. Often, at the last minute, they would have to cancel family vacations because Miguel would have to work. He imbued the household with an exemplary work ethic, and the kids learned to set their vacation expectations accordingly.

Miguel's own father and uncles had emigrated from Spain to Cuba and started a lumber business in Santiago de Cuba, on the south coast near Guantanamo Bay. At an early age, Miguel was made to haul wood at the mill, no matter how early in the morning or how hot the sun. When Castro came to power, the lumber mill was closed by government decree. "We lost everything," Miguel said, and the experience bred in him a fervid immigrant's patriotism for his adopted home. "You come in and the sky's the limit," Miguel said. "That's what this country allows, and I'll forever be grateful for that."

Jeff had another sky's-the-limit role model in his grandfather, Lawrence Preston Gise. "Pop" Gise worked on space and defense technologies for the government and, in 1964, was appointed head of the Atomic Energy Commission's Albuquerque office. He managed a staff of 26,000 and a huge budget. Jeff spent almost every summer at his ranch in Cotulla until he was a teenager. His grandfather was his best friend, he says, the most resourceful and self-reliant person he ever knew. He had expansive notions of what was possible. Bezos was also struck by his grandfather's completely unfuzzy notion of right and wrong. He had no patience for inefficiency.

In 1968, Gise wanted to close a factory in his jurisdiction, but a group of politicians insisted that it remain open. Rather than abide an inefficient plant, which employed 2,000 people, Gise retired to his ranch.

Gise was an intellectual mentor to Bezos. He and Jeff invented things together, like an automatic gate opener that did not use electricity. He taught Jeff to weld, to lay pipe, fix windmills and bulldozers, and to castrate bulls. He took Jeff to the Cotulla Public Library, which had an unusually large collection of science fiction books. A local man had donated his big collection and Bezos read them all. Science fiction formed his early world view immensely. "It was a great way of expanding your ideas of what's possible and what's not," he says.

Gise only stoked this. He told stories about missile defense systems, outer space, the wonders of nature. He was also the subject of some of these stories. Jeff has a favorite tale. Once, Pop Gise got his thumb caught between a metal gate and a fencepost at the ranch. It ripped the fleshy part of his right thumb off, and Gise was so mad at himself, he took the part of the thumb that had come off and hurled it away. Then he drove himself to the emergency room in the nearby town of Dilley. The surgeon could not sew the thumb back together without the part that Gise had thrown away. Thus, the surgeon had to graft skin from Gise's buttocks onto his thumb.

From then on, every morning in the kitchen, Pop Gise would have to shave his thumb. "It's butt skin, so it grew hair," Bezos explained. Really, he said, who else ever shaved his thumb? It's more proof that Bezos comes from a family of pioneers.

Gise also exposed Jeff to a stringent approach to competition. He taught Jeff to play checkers and always beat him. Jackie pleaded with her father to let Jeff win occasionally. Just once. For his confidence. He was so young, it was painful to watch. But Pop would have none of it. "He'll beat me when he's ready to beat me," he would say. Eventually Jeff did, over and over.

If Pop was Jeff's mentor and idol, Jackie was his foremost protector and all-purpose support system. She ran a household steeped in board games, science projects, and storytelling. She spent hours playing with Jeff, talking to him, indulging his joys—letting him watch "Speed Racer" and the "Three Stooges" every morning, "Star Trek" every night. Each night at dinner, Jackie would commence the "Interesting Thing of the Day" game, in which everyone shared an example of something interesting that happened to them that day, or risk a quarter fine. Implicit in this was an expectation: The world was full of cool things, mini-adventures to be seized. Life need not be—nor should be—prosaic. She never collected a single quarter.

She supported Jeff's geeky hobbies and curiosities, made multiple trips to Radio Shack for his assorted projects. Often, he would omit something from his parts list, and she'd have to soldier back to Radio Shack. She couldn't stand depriving Jeff the tools to push a day's possibilities. She would do this for any of her three children, but what was obvious to all of Jeff's teachers was now becoming clear to everyone who met him: He was an exceptional child.

A MODEL

This was confirmed by a standardized test when Jeff was 8. His parents enrolled him in the Vanguard Program, a pilot program for gifted students at Houston's River Oaks Elementary School, twenty miles from their home. One of his early feats involved a teletype machine that could be connected to a mainframe computer by a modem. None of the teachers knew how to program the computer, but Jeff and a few other children figured it out. They spent hours playing a "Star Trek" game.

The Vanguard Program became a model for gifted education in Texas. It drew a procession of visitors—scholars, politicians, educators from other areas—and Bezos was inevitably trotted out as the program's prize student. Cute, precocious, super-bright, he always put on a great show.

But Jackie worried that he was spending too much time outside of class. "I was afraid that they might be pushing him because he was their little token," she says. The issue came to a head when Julie Ray, the author of a book on special education in Texas, asked if she could write a chapter on Jeff. Jackie received a call from the River Oaks principal, a woman named—no joke—Judy Judy." At first Jackie said no, this was too much. But she eventually agreed, after getting several assurances from Judy Judy. Ray agreed not to use Jeff's real name.

Jeff, identified as "Tim," was described in *Turning on Bright Minds: A Parent Looks at Gifted Education in Texas* as "friendly but serious," "courtly," and a boy of "general intellectual excellence."

"It also said I had no leadership skills whatsoever," Bezos recalls. "Hah-hah-hah-hah-hah-hah!"

As a child and young adolescent, Jeff was bullied. He was neither shy about demonstrating his brilliance to people, nor about telling them if he believed they were not brilliant. One kid hit him in the head with a lunch box, drawing tears, but no blood. Jeff once called a big tough classmate "stupid," and Stupid responded by punching him in the mouth and knocking him to the ground. Another big kid demanded Jeff's lunch money, and "he would have rather gotten beat up than forfeit his lunch money," Jackie said. Jeff got his head slammed against a soda machine for his troubles.

Jackie says the bullying never became too problematic. "You learn something from being picked on," she says. In a broader sense, however, she was concerned that Jeff was becoming too "egg-shaped." She and Miguel pushed him to go beyond his geeky comfort zone, signing him up for a youth football league—a terrifying notion to Jeff, who was small for his age and had little stick-like legs. "I was dead set against playing football," Bezos says. "I had no interest in playing a game where people would tackle me to the ground."

But he approached it as an intellectual exercise, compensating for his small stature by memorizing his team's offensive plays and defensive formations. The coach charged him with calling plays on the field. He named Jeff captain. Jeff's anxiety quickly gave way to fascination, and, more important, a craving to win. With every game his Rams won, Jeff became more competitive. When the Rams lost to the Jets for the championship, he sobbed.

In 1977, Exxon transferred Miguel to Pensacola, Florida. The move brought the possibility that Jeff, then 13 and entering middle school, would not be in a program for gifted children. Pensacola required a one-year waiting period before new kids could be admitted to their program. At least in the beginning, Jeff would have to attend classes with "average" or sub-average kids. To Jackie, this was unthinkable. She solicited letters from Judy Judy and Jeff's teachers in Houston. But the administrators in Pensacola still said no, invoking "standard procedure."

"We don't have time for standard procedure," Jackie Bezos said. She convinced the administrators to at least meet her son and review his work.

Standard procedure was promptly waived. "You just don't go away," Jackie says. "You don't go gently. You just keep trying to convince people."

EARTHLY PURSUITS

By the time he reached high school, Jeff Bezos needed to convince people he was a normal teenager. After two years in Pensacola, Miguel ascended to an executive job at Exxon and moved the family to the affluent Palmetto section of Miami, where they lived in a four-bedroom house with a pool in the back. Jeff entered Palmetto high, "the kind of school where the cars in the student lot are much nicer than the ones in the faculty lot," says Andy Massimino, Palmetto's director of student activities.

Early on, another student asked Jeff what radio station he listened to. This is always a trenchant question among adolescents, a window into musical tastes and, ultimately, a person's coolness. But Jeff Bezos did not listen to the radio or particularly like music. He failed coolness.

Next time, he vowed he would do better. "I'm obviously very lacking in this," he told his mother that night. He started listening to every radio station on the dial and memorized their formats and call letters.

Palmetto was rife with high-achieving kids, the sons and daughters of executives, doctors, lawyers. He gravitated to a group of about nine or ten elite students. They wended through their days together as a roving clique of achievers: first period, honors English; second period, honors calculus; fourth period, honors physics; science club after school. Jeff drove a blue Falcon station wagon with no air conditioning, a clunker next to his Cadillac- and Mercedes-driving classmates. His clique often gathered at the Bezos house. It was where they met before the prom and where they built the homecoming float. They called Miguel and Jackie—still in their mid-30s—by their first names. They engaged in gentle hijinks, such as breaking into the school before dawn and hanging yarn from classroom lights. "There was mischief we felt we could get away with," said Jonathan Leblang, an officer with Bezos in the Palmetto honors society. "Are they really going to suspend the top whatever of the class for doing this?"

In twelfth grade, Bezos lost his library privileges for laughing too loud. He was once cited by a police officer for "careless driving," and Miguel grounded him for a month. Jackie and Miguel mandated a relatively early 10 P.M. curfew that Jeff would often challenge but rarely violate.

"He always tried to push, to see what the limits were," Miguel told me. "I'd say, 'You gotta be in bed by 12.' and he'd say 'Why?' I'd say 'Because.'"

"There was a fair amount of teenage exchanges," said Jackie. "As quick as Jeff was at assessing the whole picture, he could ring your bell, challenge you with something, with some statement, very quickly. He was not a problem kid. He didn't get in trouble. If Jeff was ever guilty of anything, it was crimes of the mouth."

Bezos's disdain for limits reflected a bent for adventure. He fixated on outer space, an interest first stoked by Pop Gise, "Star Trek," and a NASA space camp he attended in Huntsville, Alabama. He had always been taken with far-off exploration and magical kingdoms—he had visited Walt Disney World seven times. Bezos believed that space travel would soon be a booming sector, and he wanted to start a shuttle service that would spare companies the cost of launching a booster rocket. It would travel between low Earth orbit and geosynchronous orbit, 23,000 miles up.

"Jeff was dead serious about his space tug business," said Carolyn McDaniel, a friend from high school. "He thought this thing could work, that companies would want it and that he could make a lot of money doing it. Knowing Jeff, he probably had some model scenario in his head." Bezos confirms that yes, he did, but the business proved unfeasible in the end.

Bezos also remained hyperfocused on earthly pursuits. He was fiercely competitive, winning, among other competitions, a Florida-wide science fair prize for a project on the effect of zero gravity on the common housefly. In his school career, the only competition Bezos remembers not caring about was in fourth grade, a contest to see who in class could read the most books. (He also remembers finishing "in the 75th percentile" in that contest.)

He was not unpleasant about winning. "Jeff could be hysterically funny while he was trying to beat the pants off you," McDaniel said. He seemed to take no particular joy in pummeling his competition, friends said, but it was also absolutely essential that Jeff Bezos be the one to set the standard.

He found an intellectual match in Ursula "Uschi" Werner, his first serious girlfriend and the valedictorian of the Class of 1981.

They would play the word game Boggle and argue incessantly over the legitimacy of certain words. Werner excelled in literature, Bezos in math and science, and Boggle involved an opportunity to prevail in Werner's strong suit. "Chess would have been Jeff's strength," said Werner, who is now a writer living in Washington. "We didn't even try to play chess. It would have been ugly."

Werner matriculated at Duke while Bezos completed his senior year. On Werner's birthday, Bezos arranged for 200 large signs to be plastered all over campus, "Happy Birthday Uschi," the signs said along with a detailed description of her. "Hey Duke guys, Keep Your Hands Off Her, She's Mine."

Bezos applied early action to Princeton, the only college he wanted to attend. ("Einstein was there, for goodness' sake," he said.) He suffered daily agony waiting for the mail. After he was accepted, he travelled with Werner to New York. He tried to take her to Windows on the World for dinner, showing up without reservations in jeans and a T-shirt. Upon being refused seating by the maitre d', Bezos stormed out.

He kept studying and competing in high school, despite his early acceptance to college. He realized he had a chance to be valedictorian of the Class of 1982. It was an unusually gifted senior class, with more National Merit Scholarship semifinalists that year than any other public high school in the Southeast. Bezos sized up his competition and, to bolster his rank, piled on as many honors classes as he could fit onto his schedule. He aced all of his honors classes and liked his chances.

On the day class ranks were given out, seniors were called into the principal's office, their fates inscribed on index cards. "Mine had a one on it," Bezos recalls. "And it felt very gooood . . . hah-hah-hah-hah-hah-hah!"

Bezos left Miami for Princeton, away from his family for the first time. He made a point of entering campus through the main, wrought-iron gate off Nassau Street. He planned to study theoretical physics. Like Albert Einstein and Stephen Hawking. Outer space was not yet realistic, cyberspace not yet accessible, so this would be his frontier of choice. But the dream ended after he arrived at Princeton. Suddenly, Jeff Bezos was not the brightest kid in the room.

VERY, VERY TROUBLING

One night during his freshman year, Bezos was struggling over a partial differential equation he had to complete for a quantum mechanics class. After a few hours of frustration, he and his study partner visited the dorm room of a classmate, who glanced at the equation and said, "Cosine."

"After we expressed some incredulousness," Bezos says, "he proceeded to draw three pages of equations that flowed through and showed that it was cosine." It led to a realization: There were people whose brains were wired to process abstract concepts in a very graceful way, and Bezos was not one of those people. "It was initially devastating," he says, "very very troubling."

Over time, his devastation gave way to a state of awe and a dash of pragmatism. Bezos switched his concentration to electrical engineering and computer science. He studied avidly, restoring himself safely to a realm's elite. He compiled a final grade-point average of 3.9, 4.2 in his major. (A-pluses counted as 4.3.)

Bezos took his first entrepreneurial foray that summer. He and Ursula Werner started the Dream Institute, a summer school that taught a compendium of science and literature topics to children, ages 8 to 12. They drew six students at $600 each—including Mark and Christina Bezos—and they were profitable. Bezos does not recall the venture as essential to his development, but it beat his previous summer job, working the fryer at a McDonald's on U.S. 1.

His relationship with Werner lasted three years, ending with a difficult break-up. It was the formative adolescent relationship of both of them. They owned similarly high-octane minds, but they held very distinctive worldviews. "Even though Jeff was a bigtime dreamer, he had very rigid ideas," said one friend of Bezos who attended high school with both him and Werner. "He had a tendency to get a little harsh and stubborn. Ursula was softer, more psychologically focused."

Like many college students, Bezos grappled with questions of identity. This led him back to the silent issue of his biological father. For the first time since age 6, Bezos raised the topic with his mother. One summer day he asked a series of questions, which she does not share. When he was through, he gave her a hug and said, "You did a great job, Mom." In telling the story, Jackie chokes up.

Bezos says the only time he ever thinks about his biological father is when he's asked a genetics-related question on a medical form. Or when someone reminds him of it. A *New York Times* magazine profile referred to Mark Bezos as Jeff's "half-brother," a term of great irritation within the family. "I guess it's an adequate description of our genealogical relationship," says Mark Bezos, who has a marketing consultancy firm in New York. "But as far as our familial relation, it's totally inacurate." Whenever they hear that term, he and his sister Christina ask, "Which half are you, and which half am I?"

To people who ask him today about his biological father, Jeff will shrug and declare this is "a total non-issue" in his life. Miguel is his father, end of story.

Or is it? There is a theory among Bezos's friends that a source of his drive to succeed is the need to prove himself to the man who left him behind. Somewhere, there is a man named Ted Jorgensen, someone who may or may not know that the former Jeffrey Jorgensen grew up to make history in the corporate world and amass billions.

Does this motivate Bezos? He smiles, then does a clearly nervous rendition of the laugh. "Let's just say it's nothing within my ability for introspection," he says. "It's one of those things where you'll have to tell me what I really think." He laughs again, this time with a little more ease.

Miguel and Jackie Bezos give the impression of a happy couple who have lived life well and settled comfortably into their years. They are still just in their mid-50s, and they look younger. We met in Aspen, where they spend many vacations. It was the July 4th weekend, 2000. I joined them as they were finishing breakfast at a rustic inn downtown; Lizzie Allen, who had flown in to monitor my visit, was there, too. Miguel and Jackie wore bright white tennis wear, with sunglasses resting next to their glasses of fresh-squeezed orange juice.

Over several years spent in Texas and Florida, Miguel's still-strong Cuban accent has acquired a Southern U.S. twang. Jackie looks strikingly like Jeff—almost a perfect female analogue, especially her big and round brown eyes. The eyes turned adoring when she spoke of her son, just as Jeff's did when he spoke of her. Their bond, even now, is unusually close, so much so that one former girlfriend of Bezos whom I interviewed called him a "momma's boy." She meant this fondly, but said it could at times lead to a problematic expectation that they be his caretaker.

Both Miguel and Jackie seemed slightly befuddled that I was even there interviewing them. What could possibly be relevant, let alone interesting, about the long-ago times of their son? "You look back, and it's just a very ordinary life we've all had," Miguel said. In giving answers to questions, he said, it implied that the secret to Jeff Bezos's success was foremost in his mind. Or something that he even thinks about.

Yet there is something unusual about the Bezos family experience. They are unusually close, all of them, and the relationships seem stunningly free of conflict. They still vacation together several times a year. "One of the strongest family bonds I've ever seen," says Bezos's friend Tom Karzes. "It's not a dependency thing. They just genuinely enjoy each other's company." Bezos adds: "Knowing I had a strong support network made it possible for me to do something crazy."

He was seeking something crazy—or something unusual—after he graduated summa cum laude from Princeton in 1986. He weighed job offers from several large and prestigious organizations—Intel Corp., Andersen Consulting, and Bell Labs. But he took a job at Fitel, a New York start-up that was building a global telecommunications network to settle cross-border equity sales. Bezos was Fitel employee number eleven, entering the flamboyant domain of New York finance in the 1980s. He liked the challenge and deemed the founders brilliant. He recalls looking at office space with one of them, Geoffrey Heel. It was a complicated space, the kind where you immediately get lost. When they left and got into a cab, Bezos noticed Heel drawing on a pad. "He drew the entire floor plan from memory on the pad," Bezos says, shaking his head.

"WE'RE THE MAMMALS EATING THE DINOSAURS' EGGS"

He slept on People Express planes. He shuttled across the Atlantic. At 24, he was head of customer service and software development, and those divisions were based in New York and London, respectively. For six months, he spent nearly every weekend in London and weekday in New York. People Express had two 747s that crossed the ocean, and Bezos became so familiar with them, he could tell immediately which one had the thicker foam in its seats.

It was a logistical grind, especially after Fitel recruited a large customer in Japan and Bezos moved into Tokyo's Hotel Zeneco for three months. Bezos took what he calls "a visceral physical lesson" from the experience that he would apply to Amazon: the importance of being close to the customer.

Fitel also offered an early look at how connected computers could automate a business process. Bezos, adept at both debugging code and schmoozing with clients, was part of a team that built what was essentially a mini-Internet for investors, sellers, brokers, and banks. But those clients tended to think conservatively about adopting new technology, and Fitel struggled to attract new customers. In April 1988, Bezos left for a job at a financial services powerhouse, Bankers Trust Corp., where he developed software applications for the company's pension-fund clients. After ten months, at 26, he was made a vice president. As at Fitel, however, Bezos faced resistance to the technology he was developing.

"There was an old guard inside Bankers Trust that saw no reason to change anything," says Harvey Hirsch, a former BT executive who ran Bezos's division. Bezos was not shy about advocating personal computers, but several colleagues scoffed, saying that PCs did not have sufficient memory to handle elaborate financial data.

He was not diplomatic. He frequently dubbed members of the old guard "brain dead." Office diplomacy was just politics, anyway, and what's the intellectual use of that? "He always assumed his brilliance would get him ahead," says Kelsey Biggers, Bezos's closest friend at BT and a fellow proponent of speeding the pace of change within the company. "We'd say, 'We're the mammals eating the dinosaurs' eggs.'"

Outside of work, Bezos and Biggers caroused, sometimes prodigiously. They traveled often, spending memorable nights—such as the one in Los Angeles, which included dinner at Spago, two women from a disco, and Bezos getting busted in his underwear by security guards at 2 A.M. in the pool of the Beverly Hills Hotel. On the night the Gulf War began in 1990, Bezos sipped martinis at the Princeton Club of Manhattan and was transfixed by the video game aspect of the spectacle on TV.

The more stifled Bezos felt at Bankers Trust, the more he wanted a new job. He explored starting his own company. For a few weeks in 1990, Bezos even left BT to join Halsey Minor, the eventual founder of the technology news Web site CNET, to start a personalized news service for financial professionals. Their funding fell through, however, and Bezos returned to Bankers Trust.

He was tired of being a technologist at a nontechnology company. It ensured that his role would always be subordinate to the prime mission of the company (financial services in the case of Fitel and BT). He embarked on a job search. He was seeking a job that involved "second-phase automation," which he defined as a technology application that allowed businesses to revolutionize their operations. For example, a "first-phase" automation is the push-button phone, a more efficient means of performing an existing practice. A "second phase" is epitomized by the Fitel network, a complete overhaul of how equity transactions were executed. Bankers Trust was attempting the same thing with data distribution. But in his work at Fitel and at BT, Bezos came up against cultural barriers—both inside the company and with customers—and he was eager to find a second-phase technology that people were prepared to embrace.

He said explicitly to his headhunter that he was done with financial services. The headhunter then came back and urged him to consider just one more: D.E. Shaw. It had a mystique as one of the most technically advanced financial shops in the world. The founder, David Shaw, had a Ph.D. in computer science from Stanford. He was interested in both technology and finance, and was an expert in devising new trading strategies based on complex mathematical formulas.

"I immediately fell in love with David Shaw," Bezos said, and it was enough to make him break his vow against financial services and take a job at the company. Shaw was a "true genius," Bezos said, a person unusually adept at using both sides of the brain, seeing big pictures and small patterns. Many of the business practices Bezos later adopted at Amazon he learned from Shaw, beginning with hiring. Senior job candidates at Shaw face ten interviews before they are hired. Just one out of every 400 applicants are hired. "We don't always recruit for specific positions," Shaw said. "We're happy to warehouse a truly gifted individual on the assumption that they may someday make us money."

After two years, Bezos was named a senior vice president, at 28 the youngest of four at Shaw. He spent much of his time exploring new business opportunities for the firm. Bezos spent many nights in a sleeping bag and foam pad he kept rolled up in the back of his 39th-floor office.

He still found time for mini-adventures. In 1992, Bezos and Biggers drove to New Hampshire to volunteer for President George Bush's re-election campaign. They did this mostly as a curiosity; neither was terribly passionate about politics. But they found the Bush headquarters inert and stodgy, "filled with yuppies bused in from Boston," said Biggers. They left. To pass the time on the ride back to New York, they thought up offbeat interview questions, things they might ask a job candidate. If you were in outer space and you could walk on air, what would be the first thing you'd try to invent? "Jeff was fascinated by these questions," Biggers says. He spoke of how Microsoft asked job candidates, "Why are manholes round?" Why did they do this? What could they deduce? He became fixated on how to best discover and gauge a brilliant mind. Friends say he talked about it constantly.

Bezos was also seeking a wife. He was in his late twenties, making a salary in the high six figures, and ready to settle down. He devised a principle called "woman flow," a variation on the Wall Street term "deal flow," which ensured a stream of potential deals or, in this case, miserable blind dates.

But some delicious Jeff Things happened in the process. There was an infamous night at the Princeton Club. Bezos spilled wine all over the plate of his date, this exquisite Spanish woman, Valesca. "Not a little bit of wine, like a half-inch of wine," Bezos says. But what was really amazing, Bezos declared over a decade later, was the grace under pressure that Valesca demonstrated. And her resourcefulness—picking up the entire fish with her fork and transferring it to the safety of her butter plate. "She was incredibly nice and gracious about the whole situation, too," Bezos says. But not so nice to go on another date with him. "I'm not the kind of person who grows on women quickly," Bezos says. "I grow on them slowly, like a fungus, hah-hah-hah-hah-hah-hah."

In the end, Bezos fell in love with MacKenzie Tuttle, a Princeton graduate and D.E. Shaw research associate who worked in his group. There was no mutual interest when she was hired. When it developed, Bezos was terrified of acting on it for fear of a sexual harassment claim. Finally, drawn by his laugh, she approached him. They were married at the Breakers resort in West Palm Beach, Florida, in 1993.

After the wedding, Jeff and Mackenzie moved into an apartment on the Upper West Side of Manhattan. In early 1994, Bezos began working directly with Shaw to investigate business opportunities online. After decades on the esoteric fringes, the Internet was coming mainstream with the advent of the World Wide Web. Bezos had first used the Internet in 1985, in a Princeton astrophysics class, but he never thought about its commercial possibilities until the spring of 1994 while working for Shaw.

Bezos and Shaw met for a few hours each week to brainstorm ideas. Bezos would then go off on his own and research them. He isolated twenty products that could be sold online, among them software, trading services, compact discs and, somewhere down on his list, books.

But books kept rising. They could be easily sampled online. There were about three million books in print at the time, ten times the number of CDs. The Internet's search capabilities made it easy to "browse" by author, title, publisher, and keyword—an arduous process in a physical bookstore.

Selling books online was not completely untried. In 1991, Computer Literacy Bookshops in the Silicon Valley city of Sunnyvale had begun selling to its customers by electronic mail, a viable proposition because so many of them were early adopters. Two others followed suit, BookStacks Unlimited in Cleveland and WordsWorth in Cambridge, Massachusetts.

But those were niche markets, the preserve of hobbyists. What captured Bezos's attention above all was a study that said Internet use was growing by 2,300 percent annually. It was a small bubble that had seemingly infinite room for expansion. "I didn't even believe the figure when I saw it," he recalled. "I read through the methodology, and it became clear to me that this was a reasonable methodology." Bezos's research coincided with another realization: He was ready to start his own business. He had contemplated possibilities for years, increasingly as he approached 30. He told Shaw he was thinking about starting an online bookstore himself.

They took a two-hour walk together in Central Park. Shaw told Bezos he could have a bright future at the firm if he chose to stay. But he also said he understood his desire to start his own company, something Shaw himself had done when he left Morgan Stanley in 1988. Bezos took 48 hours to make a final decision. He contemplated in a paradigm he calls a "regret-minimization framework." He imagined himself in a rocking chair at age 80, asking what he would regret more: leaving a job that came with perks like a six-figure Christmas bonus, or missing out on the chance to settle the Internet.

Bezos gave Shaw his final answer and planned a road trip.

THE MAPPED-OUT JOYRIDE

In Amazon lore, Bezos and MacKenzie set out from New York and headed West with no specific destination and veered spontaneously toward Seattle. In fact, the couple flew first to Texas to pick up Miguel's 1988 Blazer. Bezos scrutinized many factors about where to base his company before he left New York—supplier proximity, labor pools, state sales taxes, convenience of that city's airport. Seattle won, beating out Portland, Oregon, because it had a large reservoir of tech workers and it was just a few hours from the largest book distribution center in the country.

Company name? Bezos liked Cadabra, as in "abracadabra," conjuring his fondness for the magical.

"Cadaver?" asked the Seattle lawyer who helped him incorporate the company.

Bezos buried that idea and moved to his next: Amazon.com. He didn't have a single customer yet, but he loved the name. Something huge. With no specific reference to any product, it would allow him to move the business in any direction.

This is no small point in understanding the rise of Bezos and Amazon. Selling books forever seemed too limiting. Even though Amazon would be introduced to the world as an online bookstore, Bezos preferred the term "book service." "Thinking of yourself as a store puts you in a box," he says. "Services can be anything."

The company was launched in 1994 with a $300,000 investment from Miguel and Jackie Bezos and loans from his own bank account. Beyond that, Bezos scrambled to raise $1 million from twenty local investors —a major accomplishment, since Bezos knew few people in Seattle and the Internet was still unknown to most. "He came off as this likable guy with an unshakable belief in what he was doing," says Tom Alberg, an early Amazon investor and longtime board member. Nonetheless, Bezos was telling prospective investors that there was a 70-percent chance the company

88   JEFF BEZOS   Everyman, Every Man for Himself

would fail and they would lose all their money. It was a responsible hedging, but also a supremely hopeful assessment given that roughly 95 percent of all start-up companies wind up failing.

Bezos worked out of the garage of his rented three-bedroom ranch house in Bellevue, Washington. "It was important that we started out in a garage," Bezos said. "Hewlett and Packard began in a garage. This gave us start-up legitimacy." He says this with a degree of irony, aware that Amazon falls quite short of a rags-to-riches story. He could never have done this without his own or his family's money.

The garage was snaked with extension cords and cramped with a potbellied stove, three large computers, and three engineers—the founder and his first two hires. Their first goal was to show that this new industry could be self-sustaining. Growth would be steady and methodical, and funded by whatever profits the company could muster. Other outside investments would come later.

That was the traditional retail model. But the plan changed almost as soon as Amazon opened for business in July 1995. One of the engineers devised a way for a bell to ring every time a sale was made. It starting ringing almost immediately, then a little more. And from strangers. Everyone looked around at one another when the bell rang. "Is that your mom? It's not my mom. I don't recognize this person. Is that a friend of yours?" Bezos says this was one of the most emotional experiences of his life.

In Amazon's first week, the store processed $12,438 worth of orders. Within the first thirty days, it sold books to people in all fifty states—without advertising. Internet commerce was becoming a gold rush overnight. But Bezos was also aware that Internet commerce required a leap of faith by users. It's one thing to communicate with words online, another thing to supply a credit card number. He stressed that the company had to take extra measures to win that trust, such as sending instant e-mail to confirm purchases, digitally holding the hands of nervous newcomers. He also insisted on a liberal return policy of thirty days.

Above all, Amazon had to grow. On August 9, 1995, Netscape held an initial public offering—and its share price more than doubled on its first trading day, even though the company had no profits. The much-hyped IPO confirmed what was becoming clear to the Internet's first movers: The rules of starting and expanding a business—and raising money for it—were changing. This meant, to Bezos's mind, pivoting from turning a profit anytime soon. It was not a bold choice, but an obvious one, he said: "To have thought otherwise would have been management malpractice."

For a brief period late in 1995, Amazon was slightly profitable, a milestone Bezos would later renounce as "unfortunate." Profits meant stinting on marketing, advertising, and infrastructure. Now, those three elements formed a tripod supporting Amazon's new corporate mantra: "Get Big Fast." Amazon finished 1996 with sales of $15.7 million—a jump of 3,000 percent over 1995. Its losses were $6.2 million, compared with $303,000 in 1995. But by this time, investor trepidation about the Internet had succumbed to early-stage hysteria. "I would give them pieces of paper with our weekly sales growth," Bezos said, "and they would say, 'Where do we send the check?'"

He took $8 million from the Silicon Valley's flagship venture capitalist group, Kleiner Perkins Caulfield and Byers, but Bezos still owned 42 percent of his growing empire, with his family holding 10 percent more. It had the early look of a certain fortune. But traditional book retailers always loomed close. Namely, Barnes and Noble.

It was inevitable that they would figure out how to sell on the Internet—how hard could it be? At which point they would quash this upstart whose giggly founder and CEO was still spending significant amounts of time packing and shipping books himself. In an oft-quoted phrase coined by Internet guru George Colony, the company would be declared "Amazon.Toast" as soon as Barnes and Noble went online.

Bezos was unconcerned. In a secret dig at Goliath, Bezos held many early meetings with his staff and investors in the cafe of a Seattle Barnes and Noble store. In a not-so-secret dig, Bezos arranged for Amazon billboards to be driven past Barnes and Noble stores. "Can't find that book you wanted?" the signs said.

He was, however, a realist. So in late 1996, when Barnes and Noble's two top executives, Len and Steve Riggio, came to Seattle, Bezos agreed to meet with them over dinner at Seattle's Dahlia Lounge restaurant.

Most people in this situation would seize the chance to cash in a few years' work for a few hundred million dollars. You could be secure in a job well done, a risk worth taking, and a preposterous fortune to spend the rest of your life enjoying. But this wouldn't be so memorable. It would be trivial. It could lead to regrets.

"The Riggios basically said, you guys have done a great job, let's do a deal of some kind," said Tom Alberg, who accompanied Bezos to the meeting. Bezos, in a congenial way, held firm. Barnes and Noble was certainly the signature brand in bookselling, but the Internet was different. Subtext: Bezos knows how to do this, you don't. He again saw himself as a mammal eating a dinosaur's eggs.

"The Riggios were sort of like New York street fighters," Alberg said. "They started saying things like, we're going online in three months and we're going to crush you." Bezos shrugged and returned to his office.

"READY, FIRE, STEER"

In the mid-1980s, Apple's Macintosh offered a populist computing alternative to IBM, the industry colossus that Apple dubbed

"Big Brother" in TV ads. In the early 1990s, Steve Case's America Online derived motivation from the perceived hipness of its chief rival, Prodigy. Netscape's crusade to let users browse the Internet became a jihad against Microsoft when it joined the browser market in 1996. Netscape was one of numerous technology firms that isolated Microsoft as their designated Evil Empire: Oracle, Sun, AOL, Apple, IBM, Intuit, and others. They had, at various times, made a corporate imperative of villifying the world's biggest software company—usually through Bill Gates. Through their external animosity for Microsoft, these companies achieved a greater measure of internal cohesion. They became largely defined through their rivals.

Bezos never bought this notion. He tried not to obsess, or speak too much, about a singular rival, like Barnes and Noble, or the online auctioneer, eBay. He drew a parallel to high school. "In my senior year, I was very conscious of the fact that if I could get perfect academic grades, I would be valedictorian," he said. "And I worked really hard to make sure I got those grades." But even though he was aware of what Linda Fetko (the West Point-bound salutatorian of Palmetto's Class of 1982) was doing, Bezos says he took no particular delight in defeating her. "There's a parallel here," Bezos says. "I ask people to focus on our customers, not competitors."

Which is not to say Bezos is averse to sharp elbows. Two of the firms he emulated were Microsoft and Disney, two of the hardest-hitting in corporate America. Bezos says that he wanted Amazon to be an "intense" and "friendly" company, but he'd much sooner give up "friendly" than "intense."

In early 1997, Kelsey Biggers was starting an Internet business and he went to Seattle to study his old friend's company. He boiled down some of Bezos's philosophies into a memo he prepared for his staff. "Jeff believes taking calculated risks is good business," Biggers wrote in the memo. "As an example, he has forecast that in five years, Amazon will be defending itself against about twenty lawsuits a year." Bezos denies having said this.

When I asked Bezos why he turned down the Barnes and Noble offer, he became oddly quizzical that such a question could even be asked. "Because," he said, "we just wanted to build something special and innovative." Barnes and Noble might have seemed like a powerhouse, but in the context of Bezos's appetites, they weren't nearly so big as he was thinking. "Almost every single person I've met in the business world has some set of limits," said Amazon's chief information officer, Rick Dalzell. "There is some paradigm they abide by. But for some reason, Jeff's been gifted with the belief that there are no bounds."

Bezos wanted to use technology to change not only the delivery of products, but also the basic model of shopping. Amazon's engineers developed "collaborative filtering" software that would customize the shopping experience to each user's tastes. Bezos saw this as a crucial achievement. He disputed comparisons between Amazon and established retailers such as Wal-Mart Stores Inc. No matter how huge they might have seemed, bricks-and-mortar superstores were intrinsically limited. "You can subdivide the demographics of these stores into maybe fifty segments," Bezos said. But Amazon caters to segments of one—each customer, several million of them.

Once Amazon had passed a threshold of viability, Bezos proceeded with the happy desperation of a man racing the aisles of a super market, madly filling his cart before his time and money ran out. Selling out to the Riggios would have signaled a premature end to his spree. Amazon sold stock to the public on May 15, 1997. By the end of the year the shares had risen 233 percent. The media loved Bezos as much as Wall Street did. Jackie Bezos perused newsstands, found magazine stories on her son, and left them open to that page.

Nearly every story mentioned the laugh, a tidy metaphor for the company, and the Internet. It came out of nowhere, big and disruptive, and packed uncertain meaning. It was more complicated than joy. Bezos deploys the laugh to convey a range of messages. "He laughs when he's really happy, and he laughs when he's really frustrated," said Dalzell. "Sometimes I'll ask him why he's laughing and he'll say, 'Because I'd be crying otherwise.'"

As the century closed, Amazon had gone far toward fulfilling Bezos's vision of anything, anytime. It was a hallmark of his instant online empire—with 20 million customers, and growing at a rate of 84 percent year after year. "Getting Amazoned" became the code phrase for what could happen to any established business—such as Barnes and Noble—that didn't "get" the Internet. Amazon's stock price hit $113 in late 1999, up 6,500 percent from the day it went public.

Bezos filled his shopping cart with other dot-com companies, purchasing stakes in Pets.com, Living.com, Drugstore.com, and many others. He ventured Amazon into videos, tool supplies, auctions. Where was he going with all this, and what was his plan? It was a question many were asking, but few people seemed to care much about getting an answer. Or care enough to stop buying the stock. "Jeff is launching this giant cruise missile in a general direction, but he doesn't know where it is going," said Paul Saffo, director of Silicon Valley's Institute for the Future. "He's inaugurated a business model of 'Ready, Fire, Steer,' not 'Ready, Aim, Fire.'"

When Bezos was named *Time*'s Person of the Year for 1999, one analyst dubbed him the author of "one of the smartest business strategies in business history." The Person of the Year distinction ensured Bezos's credentials as an Internet pioneer and made his mom cry. It was now certified: Bezos and his superachievers had started a revolution in electronic commerce.

But how long would they be around to rule?

YO-YO TIME

Amazon reflects the "financial characteristics that have driven innumerable retailers to disaster throughout history," Ravi Suria wrote in a financial analysis for Lehman Brothers Inc. in June 2000. "The party is over."

Suria's report, which was widely read, also predicted that the company would run out of cash by the end of that year. While agreement was hardly general, the report signaled that the rules were changing again: Old indicators were being applied to Internet businesses. It marked the beginning of a long summer for Amazon. On July 25, President Joe Galli quit, leaving a void of "professional" executives around Bezos. The next day, Amazon reported lower-than-expected revenue, suffered a 45-minute outage, and was subject to another string of harsh reports from many of its former Wall Street supporters. Shares dipped to 30.

I spoke with Bezos several times that summer. The profile I was writing about him for *The Washington Post* would be published in September. It was a difficult story to do because Amazon's fortunes seemed to zigzag every day. On the day of my visit to Bezos in June, an analyst said something nice about Amazon and the stock rose.

The next day, Suria released his report and it cratered.

A few days later, analyst Tim Albright of Salomon Smith Barney issued a positive report on Amazon, and shares gained back the 20 percent they lost following the Lehman report.

Then Galli quit, and the stock fell again

Then Amazon struck some distribution deal with Toys Я Us, which Wall Street rewarded as "responsible" and the stock bounced back again.

In all, it was a typical yo-yo time in a ridiculously volatile market. But it was a summer in which core questions about Amazon were taking on urgency. Now that the shopping spree was over, could these handpicked Einsteins ever figure out how to pay the bill? Would more deals with brick-and-mortar giants like Toys Я Us follow? And did such deals spell a reining in of Bezos's revolutionary ideal?

Every Internet wiseguy had a different opinion of what Amazon was doing, or needed to be doing. And to try to capture a story on Amazon in a daily newspaper over a two-month period like this was like trying to catch a fly with chopsticks.

But it also offered a chance to encounter Bezos during a period of adversity. Such times have been rare in his life, even as he kept insisting to me that Amazon was accustomed to turmoil and skepticism. That summer, he said, was nothing compared with 1994, when he had to somehow raise a million dollars in a strange city for a crazy idea. The only thing that was different now was that people were paying attention. He was unconcerned, almost glib. "We've seen this movie before," he said. "We're sort of inured to that here."

In a July 24 interview, after putting it off as long as possible, I asked Bezos his least favorite question: When would Amazon be profitable? He has been asked this several times a week for nearly three years now. And for as weary as he was of it, he'd become impressively adept at not answering it. Bezos said that Amazon will become profitable "when (its) ratio of mature businesses is higher than new businesses." There was a long pause before, presumably, Bezos would explain what this meant. But after several seconds, all that came was "Hah-hah-hah-hah-hah-hah!"

A few days later, on July 28, Bezos wrote a memo to his staff. "We're putting a stake in the ground," Bezos wrote. "We're going to become profitable. . . . The senior team met for three days last week and created the outline of a plan that takes us to profitability in Q4 [the fourth quarter] of 2001." By that time, the memo said, Bezos expected to have sales of $5 billion, produce more than $1 billion in gross profits, and achieve "solid operating profitability."

The memo seemed to declare an end to Get Big Fast. Or did it? The company is making a big push to "Go Global," the memo also said, to capitalize on the explosion of electronic commerce in Europe and Asia. Bezos declined to comment to me on the memo but acknowledged that the efforts to "go global" and "put a stake in the ground" did seem to contradict each other.

This was emblematic of so many conversations I had with Bezos that summer. He seemed genuinely untroubled by the apparent contradictions of his plan, in that he even had a plan. "This company has never been in a better position," he said repeatedly. He sounded indifferent to the sudden rigor that was being applied to Amazon's financial predicament. He was quick to acknowledge that building an online empire is hardly an exact science, that Paul Saffo's assessment that Amazon is a study in "Ready, Fire, Steer" was basically right. Online business at that stage of history demanded risk-taking. Getting bogged down in "aiming" could only stunt innovation.

His message: Trust us. We'll figure this out.

This was why it was so important to create the highest admissions standards in corporate America. E-commerce was still in "the Kitty Hawk age," he said, and his faith in brilliance represented the ultimate long-term investment. Bezos wanted a company that could follow his life's pattern of taking what's available and pushing it to its extreme. It was a philosophy that placed Amazon's fate on the intellectual fault line between hope and hubris, the line its founder had straddled for much of his life.

Employees are more than workers; they are inventors. "The smart people we have here don't sit around thinking about what the stock market will do," he told me. "We sit around trying to figure out what the customer likes, and we give them that. . . . We have to invent on their behalf."

He cited an everyday example of what his assemblage of brilliance could achieve. A customer-service representative suggested that Amazon's site include a help page in Spanish. No one acted on her suggestion, so the rep used her fluency in Spanish to do it herself. For her efforts, the service rep received an Amazon "Just Do It" award. "We gave her a used Nike tennis shoe," Bezos says, laughing.

Bezos seemed completely at ease in his position. The master of a universe that he himself created. He was slightly weary, and maybe in some denial, but at ease, seemingly with everything.

Except one thing.

JEFF'S EVIL EMPIRE

Ravi Suria. The Lehman bond analyst was a topic that seemed to rile Bezos above all others. Suria had not questioned Amazon's performance, but its viability. This was more than intellectual gamesmanship to Bezos, not some parlor game of conflicting analysis. Here was Suria, some 28-year-old upstart, trying to make a name for himself by taking potshots at the valedictorian of e-commerce. Bezos kept complaining that Suria never even called Amazon before he issued his report.

Amazon responded to Suria's conclusions publicly, some-thing companies rarely do with analysts' reports. Spokesperson Bill Curry called it "hogwash," which Bezos later amended to "pure, unadulterated hogwash." One Amazon executive told me that Bezos would invoke Suria's name all the time, even when the conversation was elsewhere. Suria became a fixation of Bezos's. He became his Evil Empire.

Bezos made a point of telling me that Suria sent a compli-mentary e-mail to Amazon's head of investor relations on the day the company announced its quarterly earnings that July. "Wow," Bezos says, quoting Suria's e-mail, "you guys are really tightening your belts." Suria confirmed that he sent the e-mail, but maintained that the quarterly results did not in any way change his assessment of the company.

When I spoke to Bezos again the following week, he mentioned this e-mail from Suria, again. He planned to frame it and hang it in his office, he said, seemingly as a point of vindication.

In all, Amazon was the subject of many harsh reports during that period, but Suria was a recurring nag. He kept blasting away at Amazon. Bezos kept mentioning his name. In February, Bezos sold 800,000 shares of Amazon stock—worth $12 million—the day before Suria issued yet another harsh analysis. Bezos had seen a copy of the report before it was released. The Securities and Exchange Commission began an investigation of Bezos's sale for possible insider-trading infractions. He said he did nothing wrong, that Amazon's stock gained in value the day Suria's report was released, the day after Bezos sold his stock.

All the while, Bezos was changing his corporate buzz phrase, from "Get Big Fast" to "March to Profitability." The media and Wall Street changed their tunes, too. Amazon had gone from "Internet Poster Boy to Piñata," in the words of board member John Doerr.

Suria left Lehman Brothers for a better job, at Duquense Capital Management.

As I profiled Bezos, I was struck by the fervor with which so many people held their opinions of him, and of Amazon, especially as it struggled. There was a high degree of predictable *schadenfreude* in this. On the day the SEC's investigation of Bezos was reported, one friend of mine said, with some satisfaction: "I can see the headline now: 'Princeton Goes to Prison!'"

But there were also a very high number of people rooting for Amazon. They e-mailed me en masse whenever I wrote about Amazon. Usually they were customers. They had visited the site, bought a book or something, and the experience seemed overwhelmingly positive. It held an enduring sort of magic for them. It represented a kind of great first date with the Internet, or even computing in general. It was easy, and if it wasn't, Amazon was nice about fixing it.

This reaction was a testament to Bezos's success at building one of the few "lifestyle brands" of the digital age. Customers rarely feel this warmly about a dominant technology company— indeed, users of Microsoft and AOL seem to use those products and services because they feel compelled to, because they are the default brands. They have, inevitably, had multiple experiences with dropped AOL connections and crashed Windows programs. But Amazon, the singular online retail powerhouse, seemed to generate a much higher proportion of customer goodwill.

There was another side to this—the calls I received from unhappy Amazon employees, usually the low-paid ones, the cus- tomer-service reps who were driven hard by their managers to answer customer e-mail at a grueling rate. They spoke of the indif- ference they felt from Bezos, except when he saw a backup of cus- tomer e-mails, at which point he became irate. They spoke of their frustration at not being able to move into better-paying jobs at the company. "Jeff doesn't care if we work in his sweatshop or not," one customer-service worker told me. "He just wants us to answer e-mail until our fingers fall off. Or we can do something else. He'll keep laughing either way."

When Bezos came to Washington in October 2000, PR chief Bill Curry invited me to Bezos's hotel suite for a quick visit. His schedule was packed with interviews, meetings, and an awards dinner he was scheduled to attend that night. He had 15 minutes in the middle of the afternoon.

As Curry led me into his suite, Bezos lay on a big bed in an adjoining room, sprawled on his back, napping with the door open. His mouth was open, and his top front teeth were protrud- ing slightly. (It occurred to me that I'd never seen a billionaire sleeping before. They seem to sleep like the rest of us, only richer.)

Curry placed his hand on Bezos's shoulder and the CEO's eyes bugged open. Then his body whipped upward in a movement I'd never seen before: His shoulders snapped up, he sprang into a sitting position, and then to his feet—all in a single motion. For a second, Bezos's body was touching nothing except the surrounding air. He extended his hand to me as he landed on his feet with a thud.

Jeff Bezos had literally bounced out of bed.

PIÑATA

By mid-2001, Bezos was insisting that Amazon expected to be profitable by year's end. He said this roughly 6,000 times a day while Amazon's stock was down 85 percent in May from its December 1999 high.

"The company is not the stock" became the newest Jeff Thing. Amazon now consisted of twenty "stores" with nearly $3 billion in annual sales. It had 25 million customers, about 10 million more than when its stock was at its peak, although Bezos has lowered his sales projections for 2001—from $5 billion to $3.6 billion.

What's been the most difficult part of Amazon's piñata year? When I asked Bezos this in spring 2001, I expected to get the "correct" CEO answer: layoffs. CEOs can never publicly bemoan them enough, talk of how painful they are to execute. Since I'd last seen Bezos, Amazon had cut 15 percent of its workforce—about 1,500 jobs. But over lunch, he said nothing about layoffs. He had several openings and took none of them.

In one year's time—a year of SEC investigations, shareholder lawsuits, and a Wall Street freefall—Bezos had lost some hair. His eyebrows had merged. But he still did not appear beleaguered.

This is the right PR face ("We're working hard, optimistic, never better!"), but the adventure seemed as fresh and authentic as ever.

Bezos spoke excitedly of the mathematical formulas and computer models his staff was building and deploying. Their goal is to quantify how best to squeeze every drop of profit from every product Amazon sold—by streamlining inventory, eliminating "loss leader" products, killing human inefficiencies. The team was run by Dr. Russell Allgor, an MIT mathematician, and Bezos was clearly excited about its work.

One of Bezos's lifelong wishes is to be a physical explorer. "If I could have my first choice, I would be a physical explorer in the nineteenth century," he said. So much of the Earth was still uncharted. Not now, though. "Only some of the deepest parts of the ocean and some deep lakes in Russia have not been properly explored," he said. Otherwise, the whole Earth's been claimed and named. There's not a lot left to find. "All physical exploration today is contrived, like breaking a landspeed record. It's not real. You're not discovering anything really surprising."

But there are still virtual worlds left to be explored. So many uncharted parts left to discover, decipher, and conquer. Bezos says he is in a new phase of cyber exploration. He expects to be at the center of change for the next five to ten years.

Likewise, Bezos is in a new phase of life. Miguel Bezos retired from Exxon after thirty-two years. At the end of 2000, he and Jackie moved to Seattle to be closer to Jeff, MacKenzie, and their 18-month-old son, Preston, who was named for Preston "Pop" Gise, who died in 1995 at the age of 80. Bezos wakes each morning at 7 A.M. in his $10-million home on Lake Washington. He "architects" two hours each morning to spend with Preston, when Preston is at his most energetic. Preston calls his father "Da" and echoes his laugh. Bezos leaves for work at 9:30 A.M. while Preston waves to him as he drives away. Bezos doesn't return home most nights until 9:30 or 10.

He was at work when an earthquake shook Seattle in January 2001. He was meeting with four Amazon engineers on the fifth floor. Everyone dived under the table. Then, when the shaking stopped, they rushed for the exits, pausing only for a few seconds to see if the Web site still worked.

It did, but the building was damaged. The construction work needed to fix it would add two stories to Bezos's daily stair-climb to his office. That's 40 percent more exercise. No problem, Bezos says. His winning streak's still intact. No one from the building was hurt in the earthquake, except for one dumb guy—not an Amazon employee, by the way. He broke his ankle jumping out a basement window. Bezos laughs when he tells this. Something about the absurdity of a guy jumping out of a basement window.

Earthquakes make for great Bezos theater. An Act of God is a Jeff Thing. Such acts are rich in chaos, weirdness, upheaval, and ingenuity. Everybody comes away with a story to tell. "You should stay indoors, by the way," Bezos says of proper earthquake safety behavior. "The big problem is falling debris. Bricks fall, loose bricks fall."

This could be a metaphor for Internet investing.

Only writers say stuff like that, he said. "Ah-hah-hah-hah-hah-hah."

Writers always try to distill people into a single image, he says. It's pretty strange. People try to do it with him all the time, now that he's famous. It's part of the adventure of being Jeff. Even an enjoyable part, but still strange.

Also strange: As he was saying this, Bezos was in the midst of just one of these distilling moments. It was June 2001. We were in an Indian restaurant in midtown Manhattan, just finishing a meal. The waiter came over with a tray of hot washcloths. Bezos grabbed one, unwrapped it, and worked it furiously over his hands and face. And he couldn't stop. He ran the washcloth up and over his forehead, into his hair, down the back of his neck. He placed it under the front of his shirt. He massaged the top of his chest, then his left armpit. He grunted slightly. People from other tables stared, but Bezos was oblivious.

This was a Jeff Thing. He had a full-gusto expression. His eyes were closed and his head bobbed up and down. He discarded the washcloth onto the table with a satisfied flip. He left it with no regrets, sapped dry, as he rushed outside to a limousine that was waiting for him.

CHAPTER THREE

JOHN CHAMBERS

Cisco's Dream Seller

Late one night at the San Jose headquarters of Cisco Systems Inc., John T. Chambers, the company's chief executive, was strolling down a hallway, sleepily hitting a balloon in front of him.

"Hey, what's up?" said Ray Bell, another Cisco executive. "Oh, I'm just really happy," Chambers said. "Just happy," he said again. "Really happy." And he disappeared down the hallway, patting his balloon.

It was like a dream sequence emblematic of the late 1990s, at the height of the technology boom. Cisco, the world's largest maker of equipment that connects businesses and people to the Internet, was on a run that would propel its stock value to $100 billion, $200 billion, $300 billion, $400 billion, and $500 billion faster than any other firm in history. The streak culminated in March 2000, at $532 billion—making Cisco, briefly, the world's most valuable company. Chambers was hailed as the ultimate executive pleaser, pleasing Wall Street with growth and profits, customers with pampering, employees with golden stock options. He signed autographs for shareholders, some of whom had no idea what Cisco did. He was a Silicon Valley rain god, the executive personification of all the Internet's promise and prosperity, a man floating on the new-economy balloon.

Until it popped.

Then Chambers became the most closely watched executive amid high-tech's boom-to-bust whiplash in the early twenty-first century. In a matter of weeks, his company went from the bluest of the NASDAQ blue chips to the bellwether for how bleak things would get. From its high of $80.06 in March 2000 to its low of $13.63 in 2001, the company lost $424 billion in paper value. For much of 2001, that loss exceeded the total value of General Electric, Wall Street's most valuable firm.

Chambers became something of a CEO test case. Could he manage in a harsh environment? Was he a business pioneer, or a creation of the boom? As good as he seemed, or just lucky? The questions went to the heart of all the post-boom uncertainty, and to the career of John Thomas Chambers, who remained the Internet's most fervid cheerleader at a dispersing pep rally.

Like many technology magnates, Chambers was raised in suburban affluence, in a household headed by two doctors in Charleston, West Virginia.

But among high-tech captains, Chambers is an anomaly. Unlike Microsoft's Bill Gates, Oracle's Larry Ellison, America Online's Steve Case, or Apple's Steve Jobs, Chambers is neither a technologist nor an entrepreneur. While Gates, Ellison, and Jobs left college to start companies, Chambers earned three degrees in nine years and began his career at IBM. He distinguished himself as a sales genius—fast-talking, evangelical, and adamant, "probably the most dynamic technology salesman who ever lived," says former FCC chairman Reed Hundt, who has known Chambers for several years.

Sales prowess can have low-rent connotations in an industry where the brooding nerd is the ruling archetype. Salespeople are tolerated as accessories for Silicon Valley's garage prodigies. They make business contacts, not revolution. Six of the sixty people I interviewed about Chambers independently described him as "polished." Is he for real? With Chambers, "sometimes you're not sure if you're looking at a diamond or cubic zirconium," said a Cisco executive who left in early 2001.

In an industry whose icons have been defined by their iconoclasm, Chambers displays none. "I want our competitors to like us" is something he has said repeatedly, and few who have known and worked with him can recall him ever raising his voice, swearing, or, in Cisco parlance, "showing any negative emotion."

During a 90-minute interview I had with Chambers in February 2001, he said, "Treat others as you'd like to be treated yourself" nine times. He's one of the few Silicon Valley CEOs who still wears a suit to work.

Chambers's style is senatorial, more akin to Washington than to Silicon Valley. While he works in an industry long averse to government, he has strenuously courted politicians, none more so than George W. Bush. Shortly before his inauguration in January 2001, Bush hosted a group of technology CEOs at the governor's mansion in Austin. Chambers cut a madly ubiquitous figure there, zigzagging through a procession of interviews, showing up at both press conferences (the only CEO to do so), and angling his way to prominent placement in group photos. He harped on the Internet's transformative power in the world, and Cisco's role in its construction.

After one of the meetings, Chambers approached Bush. "At some point, I'd like to talk to you about a few issues that are important to us," Chambers said to the President-elect, who promptly invited Chambers to a private dinner at his mansion that night. The two men had spoken several times, including the previous summer, when Chambers hosted a fundraiser for Bush at his home in Los Altos Hills, California that raised $4 million, double the record for a Silicon Valley fundraiser. But the Austin dinner was different, "a chance for John to position himself as the New Economy's ambassador to the new administration," said his friend Duf Sundheim, whom Chambers called excitedly after his meeting with Bush.

"I talk regularly to Mr. [Tony] Blair," Chambers went out of his way to tell me. "I've had multiple meetings with President Clinton. Jiang Zemin of China. Our conversation lasted two and a half hours, which is unheard of."

Such contacts are instructive in how Chambers views himself, and how he wants badly to be viewed: as a new kind of industrial leader, the CEO as head of virtual state.

Salesman as statesman.

It is a transformation that many high-profile CEOs strive for after they achieve a certain stature in their industries—or believe they have. For many, especially introverted computer types, this is an awkward transformation. Not for Chambers. His life has been a virtual charm school, steeped in Southern manners and perfected over years in the happy-talk waltzes of American sales culture.

But it's much easier to be diplomatic in flush times. "Sometimes all a great company needs for a leader is a great salesman," said Paul Johnson, a computer networking analyst at Robertson Stephens who has followed Cisco since 1992. But a slowdown requires tough measures and places Chambers in an awkward role he had always worked to avoid: bearer of bad news.

PLEASANTVILLE

A few years ago, some Cisco executives were meeting with a group of key customers at the Ritz-Carlton in Cancun. After a raucous night out, Don Listwin, then Cisco's vice president of marketing, playfully slapped marketing director Nick Francis on the back of the head.

Francis wheeled around and non-playfully slapped Listwin in the face. Within seconds, the play fight became a brawl, with

Listwin and Francis wrestling on the lobby floor, staining the carpet with blood, and dumbfounding their customers. The fight ended with Listwin pinning Francis on the ground, refusing to let him up until Francis said, "I give."

"It was a classic instance of how competitive Cisco can be," recalled Francis, who is now CEO of Tavve Inc., a North Carolina software company. He spoke of the fracas with nostalgia and added: "Thank God John wasn't there." Listwin, through a spokesperson, declined to talk about the incident.

Like many hard-driving firms, Cisco has always employed brash, Type-A executives. But this vignette distills a basic rule of life at Cisco: The contentiousness so basic to business success must play out at a safe distance from the CEO. "When you get emotional, you're not very effective in your communication style," Chambers said, and he noted with pride that he had never lost his temper or yelled in a business situation.

"Just like Larry Ellison's and Bill Gates's rough edges are reflected in Oracle's and Microsoft's cultures, Cisco tends to be more polished, like Chambers," said Ray Bell, who has worked for all three companies and went on to be the CEO of Smartpipes, a Silicon Valley networking firm.

"He always tried to find the compromise that would make people happy," said Listwin, who left Cisco in 2000 after ten years to become CEO of Openwave Systems Inc., a wireless-software company based in Redwood Shores, California.

This is manifest in Cisco's San Jose headquarters, a sprawling cubicle phalanx with a Prozac-in-the-water feel. To varied degrees, a shiny, happy ambience is evinced at many Internet firms, but Cisco is a study in the extreme. In the cyburbia of Silicon Valley office parks, Cisco is Pleasantville. Candy bowls sit on counters. Receptionists are "lobby ambassadors." Employees' children play at a nearby day-care center equipped with webcams so their parents can watch from their desks.

Every building on Cisco's campus is an orangy beige color with green window frames. Every floor in every building has break rooms and elevator banks set in the same location. Employees work on the same kind of deskset, type on the same kind of computer, and sit in the same kind of chair. Cubicles are adorned with nods to individualism: Etch-a-Sketches, Pez dispensers, Elvis photos, and the random can of Starkist chunk light tuna. But the standard-issue trappings are geared to a happy collective. Employees wear badges imprinted with the "company vision" ("changing the way we work, live, play and learn"), tenets of "Cisco Culture" ("empowerment, teamwork, stretch goals") and "FY2001 Initiatives" ("leadership in partnering/ecosystem").

Chambers presides as Pleasantville's mayor, smiling from a procession of framed magazine covers near his office in Building 10. He regularly tours the campus distributing ice cream and sweets. He is revered by Cisco employees in the most flattering new-economy language: They speak of his "partnership mentality," his "empowerment skills," his "win–win" approach to "incentivizing" his workers. "He'll always force me to think outside the box," said Senior Vice President Sue Bostrom. "He'll say: 'Well, that's not gonna scale. How will we really be competitively differentiated if we do it that way?'"

Bostrom, whose professional lineage includes Stanford Business School, and stints at AT&T, McKinsey, and Digital Equipment Co., was on the dance card of PR-sanctioned interviews that were arranged for me during a visit to Cisco's offices in January 2001. She has bright and plaintive blue eyes that make her seem six or seven years younger than her age, 40. She made perpetual eye contact, smiled throughout the interview, and was remarkably upbeat even by Cisco's standards of remarkable upbeatness. It's always a good career move to say glowing things about your boss to reporters, but Bostrom's affection for Chambers approached idolatry. Like Chambers, she spoke with exclamation points. "At the end of the day, what John has realized is, we're here because there's some mission we're trying to achieve! Something big! And we're going to enjoy the challenge! John will often say, this will be really challenging, but isn't it really fun?!"

Bostrom gushed that one of her recent recruits decided to join Cisco because Chambers smiled for 50 or 75 percent of their interview. When I asked if she had a telling anecdote she could share about Chambers, she thought for a second and stared at the floor before she smiled widely and nodded with a satisfied look of revelation.

Yes, she did have a good anecdote.

It happened a few months earlier. She was scheduled to give a speech at the Churchill Club in San Francisco to a group of 1,000 Cisco employees, media members, technology analysts, and, generally speaking, smart business types. The topic was: how companies could save money by streamlining their operations by using the Internet. Chambers spoke before Bostrom and would introduce her. They drove up together from San Jose in Chambers's blue Jaguar convertible. She was anxious and told Chambers she would do her best.

Before the program began, Chambers walked up to Bostrom backstage and looked intently at her. "You know, Sue, I know you're really nervous about this," she said Chambers told her. "But when you get up there, what you might want to do is just take a minute and think about the opportunity that you have. And that Cisco has. And just enjoy that. Just think, we're at a special place in time. The customers need a certain thing, and we have this opportunity to share this information with them. And think about how special that is."

Bostrom gave her best presentation ever, she said. She got a standing ovation. *Forbes* wrote about her. She was almost wistful at the retelling.

As I left Bostrom's office, she urged me to "Have a great day," as did nearly everyone I met that day at Cisco.

A CALIBRATED SENSE OF WONDER

Cisco Systems began in 1984 as a husband-and-wife team of Stanford University professors Leonard Bosack and Sandy Lerner. They invented the "router" as a device to allow the university's computer systems to interact. Routers serve as traffic cops along computer networks, analyzing the "packets" of data moving through and directing them to the best path to their destinations. Cisco was an instant hit.

Chambers took over as CEO in 1995, as the Internet was rushing into the mainstream of American life. While routers and Internet "switching" equipment still account for 75 percent of Cisco's revenue, Chambers has moved the company into other markets—apparatus for fiber-optic networks, and wireless devices and telephones. He has built Cisco into the dominant provider of the unseen "plumbing" for communications tools.

Under Chambers, Cisco has bought over seventy companies and absorbed them in an elaborate integration ritual. Overnight, a team fills the acquired firm's copying machines with Cisco letterhead. A Cisco sign is hung on the building, and sometimes the building is repainted in Cisco teal. The coffee in the break room is replaced by Superior coffee, Cisco's brand of choice. Employees from one acquisition wore T-shirts that said, "We've been assimilated."

Around the Valley, Cisco is known as "the Borg," a term that's also been applied to a handful of dominant and fast-growing companies or organizations—Microsoft, Oracle, and Intel. It is a reference to a "Star Trek" race of half-machine, half-humanoid drones joined in a vast "hive mind" under the control of a single authoritarian ruler. Borg spaceships wander around the galaxy forcibly absorbing other civilizations, destroying their free will, and turning them into automatons. The cold, mechanistic chant by which the Borg announce their arrival—"We are the Borg. . . . You will be assimilated. . . . Resistance is futile."—has entered the lexicon of technologists everywhere.

At Cisco, assimilation starts with Chambers, whose endeavor is to ease all the friction from the disruptive process of acquisition. His negotiating style is described as "solicitous" and "smooth." If merger negotiations reach a level of unease, which they inevitably do, Chambers will often invite his CEO counterpart for a private talk outside, at which point he will deploy his mastery of business body language—the soft hand on the back; the slow, avuncular walk; the Clintonesque knack for knowing when eye contact is required to drive home his sincerity. He also has a proclivity for breaking an impasse by focusing the conversation on points of agreement. "John is the ultimate closer," said Carl Russo, CEO of Cerent, an optical networking firm that Cisco acquired in 1999. "He is always working an agenda, moving things forward. . . . You can't leave a meeting with John without having an agreement of what you've just agreed upon and what you're gonna do next."

Russo said Chambers had superb "empathy skills," which he called "the crucial trait in all successful salespeople." Chambers is a "great accommodator," said a top executive of another Cisco-acquired company. This is a notion underscored by the generous prices that Cisco has paid for companies. It paid $6.9 billion in stock for Cerent, which had not held its initial public offering yet. At the time, the largest acquisition of any private company was $900 million.

Yet, in a sales setting, Chambers "is utterly relentless," said WorldCom Vice Chairman John Sidgmore, the recipient of a Chambers sales pitch that lasted several hours in 1999. It began over dinner at Washington's Red Sage restaurant when Sidgmore happened to mention that WorldCom was suffering outages on their network. Chambers then launched into a sales pitch for Cisco's equipment that lasted through the two-hour dinner and into the Bruce Springsteen concert they attended afterward at the MCI Center. "We were in this suite, and he had me up against a wall," Sidgmore said. "The other people there were sort of freaked out."

Even in one-on-one situations, Chambers speaks in buoyant proclamations, riffing hyperbolically with matter-of-fact assurance. The first time I interviewed him was in the summer of 1999, a time of fevered enthusiasm for the Internet, not to mention the stock prices of its juggernaut firms. We met in his office, a cramped space adorned with family photos and a Duke University basketball poster, and scattered with several recent magazines that featured him on the cover. Chambers delivered a passionate speech to me on "the New Internet Economy," using a lot of the same phrases he had in an appearance he'd made in Washington a month before. "We can be the one company that can change the world," he was saying. "It's maybe the first time there's ever been such a company." Chambers struck me as unusually ecstatic that day, but I'd never before seen him up close.

"We can be the one company that can change the world," Chambers was saying to me again the next time I saw him, at his home in February 2001. "It's maybe the first time there's ever been such a company."

What about Microsoft or Intel? No, they changed the technology, he said. They "didn't change the way we worked, didn't change the way we played, didn't change the way we lived, didn't change education," he said. "Cisco is in the position. This is the Internet revolution."

Chambers spoke with a calibrated sense of wonder, as if he were sharing these ideas for the first time, as if Cisco's shares hadn't dropped 13 percent on the day this conversation took place.

Ellison, top left, with classmates at South Shore High School in Chicago.

Ellison, with his first wife, Adda Quinn.

Ellison delivers his keynote address at Comdex, November 13, 2000 in Las Vegas.

Jeff Bezos as a high school senior

JEFF BEZOS

Bezos demonstrates an educational toy "Gus's Guts" to talk show host Jay Leno.

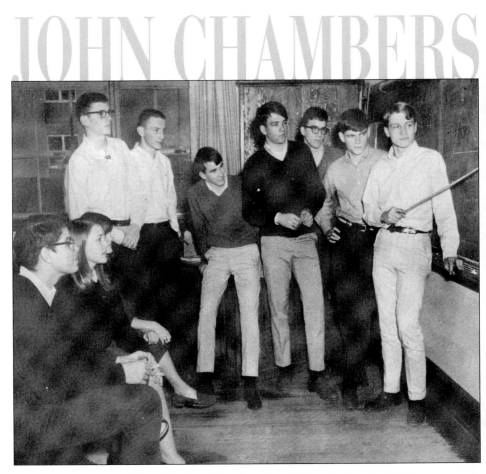

John Chambers, at blackboard, helps fellow members of the school math club figure out a problem

John Chambers, as a high school
senior in Charleston, West Virginia

Chambers, on a boyhood vacation with his family in
Vero Beach, Florida

BILL GATES

Bill Gates at 13, standing with classmate
and future Microsoft co-founder Paul Allen
(seated)

Steve Ballmer in his high school
yearbook

A young Bill Gates

Gates with Steve Ballmer, his longtime corporate alter-ego, in 1985.

Steve Case, approximately
age 5, growing up in Hawaii

The Case children in the 1970s, from left, Steve, Jeff,
Dan and Carin

STEVE CASE

Case, with mike in hand, performed a one-night stint with his Williams College band,
The Vans

NAÏVE FAITH

Chambers lives on a small private road called Via Feliz, "Happy Way" in Spanish. His house is a typical Silicon Valley new-money Xanadu, with an intercom at the wrought-iron front gate and a pool in the back. He greeted me at my rental car, shook my hand, and made the requisite inquiry on whether I found the place without a problem. He gave me the soft-hand-on-the-back as he led me to his front door.

Inside, everything was arrayed just so. Bright yellow bananas—about twenty—lined a kitchen counter. The toilet paper in a downstairs bathroom was folded into a crisp triangle. The den shelves held impeccably aligned books, including *World Book* encyclopedias, a Spanish dictionary, an unauthorized biography of Bill Gates, and separate photos of Chambers with Presidents Clinton and Bush.

Like many charismatic leaders, Chambers is easy to be with and difficult to know. The interview was planned as a relaxed, casual meeting in his den over Diet Cokes. Chambers, who is six feet tall and has thinning, wavy blond hair, wore bright white running shoes, new jeans, and a blue dress shirt. He sat cross-legged in a corner chair, a few feet away from where Cisco public relations aide Kent Jenkins was monitoring our relaxed and casual conversation.

I thought it was a good time to meet Chambers. Perhaps I'd get to see the unflappable man flustered. The day before, he had announced that Cisco failed to meet Wall Street's expectations for the previous quarter. This had never happened in his six years as CEO.

He struggled to sleep that night, he told me later. He managed five hours, waking at 6. He rode his basement treadmill from 6:15 to 6:45 while watching CNBC. At 7, he left for work in his Jaguar and listened to thirty-five voice mails from his car phone on the 30-minute ride from Los Altos Hills to San Jose. At the office, he made a series of rigidly timed phone calls, hosted a breakfast for Cisco employees with birthdays that month, walked the halls, and stoked morale. He returned home by 5:30 to meet me, ebullient again.

"I believe we're two quarters ahead of everyone else as far as understanding the issues," Chambers said a few minutes into our discussion. "When we said this economy is dropping faster than anyone understands, most people didn't grasp what we were saying in December. But our customers were telling us that." Chambers, who speaks in a high-pitched Southern accent that sounds slightly effeminate, never clears his throat and almost never says "Uhhh." He has a batch of favorite words that he uses often and pronounces like this: "pay-shin" (passion), "im-par-ment" (empowerment), "cain-didly" (candidly), and "idjic-ayshin" (education). He often punctuates his sentences with the first name of the person he's speaking to. ("Caindidly, I have a payshin for idjicayshin as a means of imparmint, Mark.")

Chambers blamed Cisco's struggles on "macroeconomic" and "outside" issues. As he often does, he posited himself as a kind of private-sector minister of economic information—a cachet acquired from his elaborate contact with corporate customers and Cisco's advanced systems for analyzing "real-time" data. This is a recurring Chambers theme: that the power of "the network" exceeds the traditional abilities of government. It falls upon him, leader of the "network revolution," to unite the two bifurcated species of the digital age: the people who "get it" and the people who don't.

Nothing seems to excite Chambers more than his dealings with world leaders. He recited a fast list of the meetings he had taken recently: with United Nations Secretary-General Kofi Annan, Chancellor Gerhard Schroeder of Germany, Prime Minister Jose Maria Aznar of Spain, Prime Minister Atal Bihari Vajpayee of India. They want to meet with him, he said, because their ability to prepare their countries for the "new Internet economy" will enhance the standard of living in their countries—"and, candidly, those people's ability to stay in power." Likewise, Chambers's imperative is simple. If he can inspire a foreign leader to invest national resources in network infrastructure, Cisco's market stranglehold is such that it is practically guaranteed substantial contracts.

Plus, in a more pedestrian sense, Chambers appears awed by these meetings. "Who would have thought someone from West Virginia would be running Cisco?" is a refrain, asserting his small-town humility while underscoring the high-level company he's keeping.

Chambers's self-ruminations are stubbornly upbeat. He called his father his "best friend," his mother "wonderful," and his two younger sisters "great." His two children, now grown, are "fantastic." Of Elaine, his wife of twenty-seven years, he said, "The longer we're married, the closer and closer we get."

He betrays no complications or anything like angst. He stays on-message, carries a thick briefing book for that day's meetings. While many executives do this, Chambers's reliance on his book is striking. At the Davos World Economic Summit which he attended in January 2001, the book was five inches thick, and he spent eight hours a night drilling himself for the next day's meetings. He prefers tidy synopses to heavy helpings of data. He delivers speeches without scripts, memorizing key points beforehand.

Friends and Cisco's PR staff strain to emphasize how modest Chambers has remained as a celebrity CEO. Although his 2000 compensation totaled $157.3 million in salary, bonus, and stock options, humility is a principal theme of the Chambers brand. He doesn't have his own parking space, friends and associates note; he washes his own car, he always holds doors open, he greets support staff, he eschews the honorific "Mr.," and takes out his own trash. "My office is twelve by twelve," he said. "We don't build monuments to ourselves." Everyone at Cisco flies coach, he said, though Chambers pays for a Falcon 2000 jet for his own use.

An avid tennis player, Chambers often strains to point out that he only plays doubles. It shows that he's much more attuned to team achievements than individual ones. "The first time we played together, I hit the first three balls into the net and John explained to me why it was his fault," says Duf Sundheim, a Palo Alto lawyer who is Chambers's doubles partner each Sunday at the University Club of Palo Alto. Chambers, he said, is a tenacious net player who is exceedingly generous on line calls. In ten years playing with him, Sundheim has never heard Chambers swear or scream. He once spent 15 minutes hunting for a lost ball in some bushes. This is not normal CEO modesty, Sundheim said.

But Chambers cares deeply about his public image. He has worked hard to position himself in the firmament of tech leaders—Gates, Jobs, former Intel chief Andy Grove—and few CEOs have received better press coverage. He became a cover boy of a New Economy magazine genre whose enthusiasm for Internet businesses mirrored Chambers's own brand of breathless gentility.

When he first became CEO, Chambers was blissfully unaware that the media could be anything but a conduit for his sunny message. After one interview with *The New York Times*'s Larry Fisher in 1995, Chambers smiled earnestly. "Larry," Chambers said, "I hope you'll let us see a copy of the *ad* before it's printed." Fisher doesn't recall this exchange, but the Cisco PR official who sat in on the interview does vividly.

The misstep reflects how Chambers views the world. "John has a lovably naïve faith that he can inspire anyone, anytime," said a Cisco executive who left the company last year. Chambers figures if he prepares enough to master his material and hone his pitch, he can win over the most cynical audience.

Chambers studies diligently for even the most casual contact with the media. In preparation for our interview at his home, Kent

Jenkins prepared Chambers an elaborate paper for Chambers on what to expect during our relaxed and casual conversation. It was part of that day's thick briefing book, which happened to be resting on a footrest next to where Chambers was sitting. I asked if I could see the page devoted to my visit in his briefing book. We had been talking about how much he relies on his book, so I figured it was relevant, if slightly self-centered. But Chambers clearly wasn't accustomed to a request like this.

He hesitated. He opened the book to my page and studied it, making a quick judgment of whether it contained anything sensitive or that would hurt my feelings. Then he passed it to me.

"Uhh, let's not do that," muttered Jenkins, who was suddenly staring at his lap. Chambers overruled him, saying that my right to view my briefing paper was consistent with his belief—and Cisco's belief—in openness. Information wants to be free.

The paper included four headings on a single page—"thumbnail," "key issues," "reporter background," and "likely questions"—with bulleted points listed beneath them. It also contained several impressions I had shared with Jenkins in a series of off-the-record talks we'd had in previous weeks. "Mark thinks you're a bit of an enigma" was one thing I recall the paper saying. After I handed him back his book, Chambers cackled, nervously, hoping I wasn't offended. He then smiled, and Jenkins smiled, and I smiled, and Chambers told a joke about something or other and the moment passed and the message was reinforced:

This man is happy.

"I think people at times struggle with John," said Carl Russo, now a Cisco group vice president. "Because he's so relentlessly positive, people wonder, is he actually human?" One friend spoke admiringly of Chambers's "genuine polish," attuned to the seeming contradiction.

"I think," Russo said, "that the veneer and the substance are a lot more closely aligned in John than any of us know."

FRIENDS FOR LIFE

"I can do it, I know I can do better," Johnny Chambers would say. He was the most determined student his tutor had ever worked with.

He was 7 and couldn't read. "Small" read like "llams" on the blackboard. "John thought he wasn't as smart as the other kids," said his father.

Worse, he thought he was stupid.

Few knew the word "dyslexia" in 1950s West Virginia, but Lorena Anderson did. She was an early expert in the field of learning disorders who lived near the Chamberses' home in Charleston. John visited her at her home after school. She taught him to read by feel, not phonics, drilling him to move his hand left to right on a plate of sand. She kept repeating "left to right, left to right," and would drag his hand from left to right with a crayon on a newspaper. Some nights, after particularly tough days in class, John would call her at home, seeking support and advice. "The kids who can stay positive are the ones who get through this," Anderson said.

"I didn't have a good day today," the blond, blue-eyed, and grinning Johnny would often say when he arrived at Anderson's home. "But it was a better day than yesterday."

Chambers does not portray his dyslexia as scarring. He plays down the teasing it brought. But people close to him say it was a critical experience, an early source of the blazing ambition that would mark his career. He vowed to outwork and outprepare everyone else to avoid the daily humiliation he faced in class. It wasn't enough to simply learn to read; he needed to become the best reader in class. "When you learn to overcome an experience like that, you feel like you can do anything," Chambers told me.

Chambers rooted for the nearby Cleveland Browns and admired the Boston Celtics for their teamwork and dominance. He competed fiercely at basketball on the family driveway and in

Charleston's church leagues (he is a Methodist). "John always remembered when he lost," said a neighbor, Jim Buckalew.

The Chambers family lived in a flat, tree-lined neighborhood of ranch and Tudor-style homes in the Kanawha City section of Charleston. It was all "a Donna Reed, 'Leave It to Beaver' world," said Buckalew, one of Chambers's three closest friends. They went through Cub Scouts, double-dated at the bowling alley, hunted fowl, fished for bass, and caught bullfrogs at the Chamberses' summer home on the Elk River. They rode together with their dates to the Charleston High School prom (held in the school gym), then met up afterward at the party at John Walsh's house on the west side.

June Chambers, a psychologist, was an outgoing and attentive mother who brought hot glazed doughnuts home to John and his sisters after school. John's biggest influence was his father, Jack, an obstetrician-gynecologist who delivered 6,500 babies in a practice that served numerous prominent Charleston residents, including the family of Senator Jay Rockefeller. He dabbled in health-care ventures and Republican politics (once running unsuccessfully for the state Senate). Affable and enterprising, Jack Chambers ran his household as John would lead Cisco: with an ethic of achievement, in an atmosphere devoid of confrontation or open rebellion. It was a home free of rules, with a few exceptions: The kids were not allowed to go steady—"I didn't want them to miss out on the fun in life," Jack Chambers said—and under no circumstance could they ride motorcycles. To reinforce this second rule, Jack arranged for his son to spend a summer working in an emergency room.

John strove to please his parents, who placed a premium on his education. He enrolled at Duke University, then transferred to West Virginia University after two years to join his high school prom date, Elaine Prater, the only person outside his family he ever told he loved. It was the late 1960s; Chambers spent most of his free time in college playing and organizing intramural sports. He kept his hair medium length and expressed irritation at the anti-war protests that were building on the nation's campuses, including Duke and WVU. His political views were conservative and he supported the war, but not what he believed was the halfhearted way it was being fought. "If you're going to fight a war, and you're going to ask young people to go, you fight it to win," he said. "It's a little like business." A bad ankle spared him from military service.

Chambers enrolled in law school at WVU and once again carried on a long-distance relationship with Elaine, who was working on a master's degree at Memphis State. They had dated on and off for seven years. Chambers was always more hesitant to commit to her, a vestige of his father's "no going steady" dictum, but by his second year of law school, Chambers began missing her terribly. He called Elaine one day and asked her to return to West Virginia to live with him. She responded with an ultimatum.

"Let me explain it to you," Elaine said. "I'll come back and marry you, or I'll find somebody else."

"I worded that wrongly," Chambers said. "Would you marry me?"

Shortly after he started business school at Indiana University, Chambers married Elaine. Jack Chambers stood as his son's best man. After a reception at the Edgewood Country Club in Charleston, John and Elaine honeymooned in Las Vegas.

In 1976, Chambers took a sales job at IBM. He was reluctant to work in sales, feeling that his law degree and MBA training suited him better to marketing or operations. But the branch manager, Chris Christie, convinced him that computing—in which Chambers had shown little interest—was changing the world. "He was the first one to get me excited about computers," said Chambers, who came to seize on a central tenet of IBM's sales culture: The company wasn't selling products as much as it was selling dreams—dreams of a business process made more efficient by IBM computers. It was a philosophy that allowed Chambers to peddle hope and possibility, which was far more exciting than the widgets he was actually selling.

He was trained in classic sales techniques and absorbed the methods of IBM's master salesmen—their language (say the person's name), their attentiveness (always drive toward a deal, always follow up), their sense of invincibility (who else would you buy from but IBM?). He also embraced IBM's code of appearances: pressed suits, impeccable manners, crisp presentations—a universe removed from the T-shirted entrepreneurs in 1970s' Silicon Valley. Chambers worked for IBM in sales offices in Indianapolis, Pittsburgh, and Cincinnati.

He was promoted steadily but stunted by IBM's slow-moving and cautious culture. His immersion in the field told him that the computing marketplace was moving faster than IBM was. In the early 1980s, Chambers was called to IBM's Armonk, New York headquarters to discuss his career prospects with an IBM executive. "If you don't mess it up, you have great potential here," the executive said. But he urged Chambers to focus on doing one or two things really well instead of ten. "That, to me, was a way of expressing that IBM was not successful," Chambers said. "You were rewarded for being status quo." It was one of many such examples that frustrated Chambers at IBM. His frustration grew as IBM was getting blindsided by the advent of smaller, cheaper "personal computers" introduced by upstart firms such as Apple Computer Corp.

Chambers left IBM in 1982 to join Wang Laboratories, the old-line mini-computer power based in Lowell, Massachusetts. There, Chambers became a protege of founder An Wang, the quiet, Chinese-born engineer. They shared a love of tennis and bridge, and played often. They spent far more time together than vice presidents usually spend with CEOs, especially CEOs who are decades older. Moreover, An Wang's son, Fredrick Wang, also worked at the company, eventually becoming its CEO. But he was not particularly excited about business, and Chambers was seen by some as a kind of surrogate son to An Wang.

An Wang moved Chambers through a series of critical sales jobs. Chambers became the first non-Asian at Wang to run the company's Asia–Pacific sales operation. In several positions of increasing responsibility—both at IBM and Wang—Chambers never missed his sales targets.

Chambers schmoozed prodigiously with his customers. He traveled all the time. On September 6, 1985, he was flying from Madison, Wisconsin to Milwaukee on a clear afternoon. The woman next to him was visibly nervous about flying. "Don't worry, my wife's afraid also," Chambers said, and he comforted her with statistics on how rarely plane crashes occur. Upon landing in Milwaukee, Chambers changed planes to head to his home, then in Boston. The woman stayed on the same Midwest Express plane, bound for Atlanta. Chambers watched her plane climb 700 feet, then explode into flames and crash nose-first in the woods south of the airport, killing all thirty-one people aboard. "Ever since then, my palms have sweat on takeoff," Chambers said.

This was not a life-altering trauma, Chambers said. It was worse for him a few years later, when Wang Laboratories was in a death spiral of its own. The company was ambushed by PCs, just like IBM. Even as Chambers's career trajectory rose through the 1980s, Wang's sales fell. It set the stage for what Chambers called the low point of his career: the task of laying off 5,000 workers.

An Wang called Chambers back from Asia to run the U.S. sales operations in the spring of 1988. Chambers asked if he could return that summer. No, Wang said, he was needed the next day. That's when Chambers knew the situation was bad. The layoffs occurred over a fifteen-month period in 1989 and 1990. "It seemed like every holiday except Christmas we were planning a new layoff," Chambers said. While no executive enjoys a layoff, the Wang experience was a searing one for Chambers, his friends say. "It absolutely ripped John apart," said Selby Wellman, a former IBM and Cisco executive. "He told me, 'If I ever have to do a layoff at

Cisco, I'll lay myself off.'" Jack Chambers said the Wang layoff was the most difficult experience of his son's life. "If John has an Achilles heel, it's that he's too sensitive," he said. "He's always thinking about who is hurting. Maybe too much so."

Current and former colleagues say Chambers can be overly dedicated to people under him. "He tends to trust too many people for too long," said Nick Francis, which can breed, in the words of one former manager, "a high Bozo factor" at Cisco, meaning that Chambers is willing to carry a proportion of low performers at high levels out of personal loyalty. "John believes a lot of the time that the team that got you there is the team that can get you to the future," Don Listwin said.

"I make friends for life," Chambers said, and it's as much a professional philosophy as a personal one. In 1990, shortly after the March 24th death of An Wang, Chambers was despondent in his job. His father said, "John, if you're not happy with what you're doing, please change it," and John swiftly quit Wang Laboratories and spent a month sending out résumés. This yielded no interviews but sparked a revelation. "You realize how the world works" on friendships made and kept he said. Chambers contacted people he knew from every station of his career: colleagues from Wang and IBM, school pals, friends of friends, relationships he'd forged in his considerable travels. He drew interest from twenty-three companies, twenty-two through old friends. He was steeped in the force of his professional network, the only kind of network he knew—until he joined a company that was building them for computers.

PLEASING

Cisco's co-founders Bosack and Lerner left the company in 1990, shortly after its initial public offering. They clashed with the company's new management team, led by a blunt and seasoned high-tech executive named John Morgridge. Morgridge learned about Chambers from Cisco executive Terry Eger, an old Chambers friend from Wang. Chambers had been focusing his job search on larger technology companies, but he was drawn to Cisco in part because Morgridge told him he planned on stepping down as CEO soon and Chambers could be in line to replace him.

Chambers was hired in 1991 as Cisco's senior vice president of worldwide operations and became CEO four years later. His strategic philosophy followed closely on a lesson from his IBM days: that successful companies in fast-growing markets must be fast, bold, and hyperambitious. He became a super-salesman for the dream of the connected world. "John just had a crystal-clear vision of the great blue Pacific of data networking," said Reed Hundt. "He just marched into it, like Balboa."

As at IBM, Chambers's sales pitches included the implicit message of dominance. Just as IBM was seen as *the* computing firm in the 1970s, Chambers sold Cisco as the Internet company in the 1990s: Buy Cisco, bet on the Internet.

Chambers assumed a manic regimen of speeches, high-level meetings, and media appearances from Cisco's on-site TV studio. "We're in the midst of the second Industrial Revolution," he'd say, noting how the Internet's rate of acceptance was six times faster than phones and how daily volume of e-mail in the U.S. already exceeded traditional mail.

For all his lofty notions, Chambers's most celebrated executive qualities stemmed from his basic pleasing skills. He solicited employees' viewpoints, kept abreast of their personal predicaments—whose mom was sick and who was contemplating a new job—and oversaw one of the lowest attrition rates at a major technology firm. Cisco was consistently rated one of America's best companies to work for.

Several employees recall an event where Chambers was at his kindly best. He was hosting a question-and-answer session with a group of kids in connection with the company's "bring your children to work day" activities in 1997. An 8-year-old girl got up to ask a question. She held a microphone, stammered for several seconds, and started to cry when she couldn't get her question out. It was clear she had a developmental handicap of some kind and Chambers honed in. "I can identify with that," the CEO said. "I have a learning disability, too." He told her about his dyslexia, something he had never discussed publicly before. "Go slower," Chambers said to the girl, "because I know when I'm excited, I don't do as well." The girl asked her question, and Chambers, who has spoken often about his disability since then, received several dozen supportive e-mails from his employees afterward.

"John doesn't pretend to be a visionary or a business operations genius," said Paul Sagawa, a networking analyst at Sanford Bernstein. "What he's great at is talking and listening to people."

"I make my life reading people," Chambers told me. "I can read an audience, read an individual. And I rarely miss."

He applies this skill to Cisco customers, for whom he is known to be obsessively attentive. Each night, he receives voice-mail updates on Cisco's "critical" accounts; he devotes 30 hours a week to time with customers and ties employee bonuses to customer feedback.

If Chambers has the occasion to criticize someone who works for him, he will do it privately—and gently. "He'll tell you three good things about you, then he'll unfold the message," Listwin said. At a roast for Chambers at his fiftieth birthday party in 2000, Listwin introduced the concept of a "Chambers Secret Decoder Ring." This was a translation device in which the seemingly glowing things Chambers said were "decoded" into his intended criticism.

Chambers also made an art form of pleasing Wall Street. Cisco beat analysts' expectations by one penny a share for fourteen consecutive quarters. A $600 investment in the company at its 1991 low would have appreciated to $82,000 at its high in 2000. At its peak, Cisco's shares had risen 100,000 percent from its IPO in 1990. Cisco could essentially print its own Monopoly money by issuing new shares. They would use this home-brewed currency to shop for promising networking firms, twenty-two in 2000 alone. It's a great way to please customers and attract new ones, in addition to saving billions on research and development.

By cultivating a style and building a culture based on pleasing, Chambers believes, a company can transcend a range of obstacles. That, as much as anything else, sums up his business philosophy. He is adept at seeing problems and opportunities and acting quickly. "It's not that this company's the world's most proactive company," said Carl Russo. "What it is is a great reactor."

The strategy reflects another central Chambers code: He has no interest in tying Cisco to a signature innovation, as Microsoft is tied to Windows or Apple is to the Macintosh. He calls himself "agnostic" on technology. Cisco will simply build, or buy, the technology that will most please its customers.

By the end of 2000, Cisco was either first or second in its share of the fifteen network equipment markets it was in. Roughly 75 percent of all Internet traffic traveled by way of Cisco products. The global network was doubling in size every one hundred days—and Cisco was enjoying a parallel explosion. Its revenue grew by 25 percent or better between 1991 and 2000. Just one other company has ever delivered over fifteen consecutive years of over 20-percent growth—IBM in the 1960s and 1970s.

Cisco also became a model for using the Internet to cut its own corporate costs—saving $1 billion a year, Cisco declared. It developed an online reporting system that allowed it to close its financial books in a single day.

As the company grew, Chambers began to focus on pleasing a new constituency: government. It loomed as a potential obstacle that has stymied other dominant but less pleasing tech firms, notably Microsoft. Cisco's market position and business practices made it vulnerable to regulation: Its enormous market shares could invite antitrust scrutiny; its acquisition strategy could be hindered if the Securities and Exchange Commission set more stringent rules by which companies must account for their mergers.

Chambers first bore into politics in 1996, when he joined other Silicon Valley executives to defeat a California ballot initiative that would have made it easier for shareholders to sue companies. Since then, he has redoubled Cisco's lobbying activities and courted influence at the highest levels.

He has given large sums to members of both parties. He struck up friendships—or "close working relationships"—with former House speaker Newt Gingrich, former New York Senator Alphonse D'Amato, California Senator Dianne Feinstein, Connecticut Senator Joe Lieberman, and others, notably, George W. Bush. Officials from both the Bush and Gore 2000 presidential campaigns asked about his interest in administration jobs, Chambers told friends. He has also been mentioned as a possible candidate for governor of California and senator from West Virginia. Chambers wouldn't talk to me about the prospective job discussions with Bush or Gore, saying only that "it's a tremendous honor" to have been considered and all that. He said he planned to stay at Cisco through 2004, and when he's done at the company, he plans to teach.

But given Cisco's struggles in 2001, Chambers's enthusiasm for high-level meetings led some company officials to ask whether he was spending too much time on politics and diplomacy, and not enough time tending to his business. The concern was relayed to Chambers on a few occasions, including one off-site meeting with Cisco executives in 2000. There, a research committee recommended that Chambers spend less time on the road and more time in San Jose running the company. Chambers was visibly uncomfortable with the implicit criticism, especially since it came in front of his management team, said Listwin, who was present. Chambers seems to disregard most criticism from people who work for him, according to one former member of his executive team. Chambers will, Listwin said, "graciously ignore criticisms he didn't think had merit," then do what he wants to do.

"I once said, 'John, you don't want to listen to bad news, you're trying to snuff out rebellion,'" said Nick Francis. "He got convulsive. He was like, 'Nick, Nick, don't say that.' It's like denial."

Chambers will always listen to Morgridge, who is still chairperson of the Cisco board. But beyond the no-brainer politics of this, there's a noticeably parental dynamic between Morgridge, 68, and Chambers. When Morgridge enters a room, Chambers always straightens up like a Boy Scout, said Cisco officials who have seen them together. Casual and blunt, Morgridge is a Chambers opposite. He was also a big supporter of Al Gore's presidential campaign.

I met Morgridge for breakfast on the morning of February 7, 2001, just a few hours before my meeting at Chambers's house. Kent Jenkins joined us. I planned to ask Morgridge if he had concerns about the volume of Chambers's extracurricular work. But he beat me to the topic, in a way that indicated it was on his mind to begin with. When I asked him why he decided to step down as Cisco's CEO in 1995, he responded with a long diatribe about how CEOs can become distracted over time. "CEOs, particularly in our industry, they like the job, but they become infatuated with all the other things," he said. "They become engaged in things that aren't right on target. They spend a lot of time on politics, or in the civic world."

It's hard to imagine a better invitation to ask Morgridge if Chambers had become too engaged in other things. "I think it's a concern in the general sense," Morgridge said, "mainly because John works very hard, and you're always concerned that your asset can get worn out." He had raised the issue with Chambers. "In the end, it's his [Chambers's] decision to make those assessments." At which point, Morgridge seemed to conclude that he probably shouldn't talk about this anymore.

Before he left, Morgridge allowed that Chambers would be a natural in politics, if that's what he chose to do. He even encouraged Chambers to run for something, and said he would support him if he did.

When I met Chambers that night, it was clear that Jenkins had briefed him on what Morgridge had said, or at least what he had strongly implied. So Chambers was prepared. He assured me that his political dealings were held to a tight schedule and tied directly to his business.

"These are not social things to do," he said. "This is my business."

BAD OMENS

Cisco's announcement of its financial results for its fiscal second quarter in February 2001 was one of the most hotly awaited business events of the year: How far had the so-called Internet Economy fallen?

Or what was left of it?

If it ever existed at all?

And who would have thought that its ever-giddy dream seller, John T. Chambers, would be looked to as its barometer of woe?

He had been on the road for weeks—China, India, Spain, Switzerland, Washington for the Bush inauguration. Sixteen- to 20-hour days. Two hours of voice-mail and e-mail before bed. Three hours' sleep. Toughest grind of his career, Chambers said.

On February 2, he was joined in Madrid by two aides, Maureen Kasper and Blaire Christy, who would help prepare for the February 6 announcement. They worked for nine hours aboard Chambers's jet en route back to San Jose. Chambers then dozed, and awakened to Kasper's stricken face. All the work they'd done was lost, she said. It just vanished from her laptop. She tried everything to retrieve it, but couldn't. Chambers took a deep breath. He remained calm—have to remain calm—because "that's how you teach young leaders," he has often said. They would try to get one of Cisco's IT whizzes to hunt down the lost data on Saturday. Failing that, they'd just come in on Sunday to start again.

Turns out, an IT guy rescued the presentation Saturday and averted a massive headache. But bad omens kept revealing themselves. On Tuesday, February 6, about 30 minutes into Chambers's conference call to announce Cisco's earnings, the phone connection was lost. Network problem, Chambers explained, "a sales opportunity." A joke. He started again from the beginning.

Cisco earned $6.75 billion in the last quarter, short of the consensus projection of $7.1 billion. Revenue for the coming quarter could drop as much as 5 percent, Chambers said. This would be Cisco's first decline after eleven consecutive years of growth. Sales to dot-coms were down nearly 50 percent, Chambers said. Orders from telecom carriers, 40 percent. The day after he made his announcement, Cisco's shares dropped $4.69, closing at $31.06.

Still: "We can be perhaps the most successful company in history," he told me at the end of my visit to his home that night. "We can be the best at giving back. . . ." He peeked mid-marvel at Jenkins. He then sprang up and extended me his hand. He said we would keep in touch. "At Cisco, we build relationships, Mark," he said, looking me directly in the eye.

He would now take Elaine out for a Mexican dinner. She deserves it, he said, after all the patience she'd shown him in the previous weeks, and he's thankful for Elaine every day, and it just keeps getting better between them after so many years.

Chambers led me out, again placing his hand gently on my back. He asked me how I thought the discussion went—and how Jenkins was serving me—before closing with a summation on self.

"What you see is what you get with me," Chambers declared at his front door, pointing the way out of Via Feliz.

HAVE WE MENTIONED
THAT HE'S HAPPY?

The next afternoon, I was back at my desk in Washington and received a surprise phone call from Chambers. He was calling to follow up.

"That was one of the most stimulating interviews I've ever had, Mark," he said, his voice echoing over a speaker phone.

But something wasn't sitting right with him. After I left his home, he'd got to thinking, had talked to Elaine and he realized he missed a few things, especially about his childhood. He didn't perform in the interview as well as he'd have liked to. There were other points he wanted to make to me, provided he could take a few minutes of my time.

First, the night before, Chambers felt he didn't draw a strong enough connection between the good sportsmanship of his childhood basketball games and the "I want our competitors to like us" philosophy that he brings to business. "I can still remember that Bill Nottingham's team beat us in eighth grade," he said, talking extremely fast. "But the second the game was over, there was a tremendously strong friendship and respect. . . . And Jimmy Buckalew used to dribble around me on the left, then hook me with his right arm and the ref would never call it." But Chambers never argued or let it bother him, and, anyway, he and Buckalew would always be great friends.

Chambers sounded more upbeat than he had the night before, which had been plenty upbeat by anyone's standards. He seemed to sense that he'd come off a little weary at the end and betrayed a touch of doubt. So he assured me on the phone: "I don't ever get down, Mark," he said. "If I do, Elaine brings me up." Or, if he gets too far up, Elaine brings him back to Earth.

But he wanted to reinforce that Cisco's "challenges" had no effect on his confidence. None. "I have no doubt," he said. "We will come out of this stronger, and the competition will come out of this weaker, and my confidence on this is absolute."

By the end of the conversation, Chambers was practically yelling.

MISERABLE

But the situation just kept getting worse, worse than anyone could have expected.

On April 16, Chambers made a staggering announcement. He said that Cisco's sales would decline as much as 30 percent from the $6.75 billion it had generated in the previous quarter. Two months earlier, he'd predicted that sales would be "flat to down 5 percent." He also said that Cisco would write off $2.5 billion for excess inventory, a deeply embarrassing measure for a company that had so trumpeted its state-of-the-art forecasting methods and efficient operations. Rates of attrition rose among Pleasantville's citizens, more than half of whom now owned stock options that were well under water.

"Cisco has never been in this situation before, and it's been tough on John," said Jack Chambers, who told me that he'd had more conversations with his son—two or three a week—than he had in years.

On March 9, Chambers said that Cisco would eliminate as many as 8,000 employees. It was the first mass job reduction in Cisco's sixteen-year history. The company's news release referred to the action as "involuntary attrition." Chambers slept a total of 90 minutes the night before the announcement.

Usually, when a company announces layoffs, Wall Street shows instant approval. But given Chambers's repeated pledge never to execute them, the market took his announcement as a sign of trouble rather than a signal of farsighted austerity. Cisco's shares dropped an additional $2.19, to $20.63.

A month later, Cisco announced that an additional 500 jobs would be cut.

Chambers was never shy about discussing the personal pain of laying off workers at Wang. It was always an expedient thing for him to talk about, an assertion of his humility, his compassion, his lessons learned. Even though Cisco under Chambers was never close to needing to cut jobs, it was doubtless a comfort to employees—and a selling point to prospective ones—that they worked for a CEO who would never oversee a layoff. He had made the promise all the time.

But as the economy shifted, it was fascinating to hear Chambers hedge his promise in subtle ways. It resembled the rhetorical finesse of a good politician.

"I'm never going to let that happen again in my life, never," Chambers told *Investment News* in November 2000.

When I interviewed Chambers three months later, as Cisco's position was deteriorating, he reiterated his no-layoff vow, but with wiggle room. "I'll move heaven and earth to avoid them again," he said, "because you wreck people's lives."

Four weeks later came the layoffs.

I spoke to Chambers again a few days later. The layoff "speaks to the seriousness" of today's economic situation. Cisco, he said, had gone from a rate of 70-percent growth in November 2000 to a negative growth rate in January and February of 2001. "No one has ever decelerated at that speed," he says. Even when he is assessing bad news, Chambers takes care to couch it in terms flattering to his company. "It goes with the territory," he said, "of being the most profitable, fastest-growing company in history."

In a 20-minute phone call, Chambers returned often to the relevant bromides. He said "You deal with the world as it is, not as you wish it to be" three times and "Things are never as good as they seem in good times, and never as bad in bad times" twice.

I asked if he had broken his promise about layoffs. "Yes, I said I would do everything I possibly can not to go through that again," he said. It was an acknowledgement, but not an answer.

Chambers told me about all the e-mails he'd been getting from his employees, including some who would lose their jobs. Nearly all of them—about 95 percent—were supportive, he said. "Mark, it would kill you," he said of the e-mails. Then his voice lost its normally smooth cadence. "I haven't failed at many things in my life, Mark," he said slowly, haltingly. "But I failed at preventing layoffs." It will be a "scar on my history."

He ended with an uncharacteristic word: "miserable."

Then, as if receiving a gift, Chambers seized an opening: I asked him again if any of this unpleasantness had doused his enthusiasm for the "New Internet Economy," and "changing the way people live and work and play" and all the things that he had gotten so excited about for the last six years. Gosh, no, he said. In tough times, great companies break away. During every revolution, there are bumps. He talks to people, listens, travels the world, sells the dream. He asked me his favorite rhetorical question: "Isn't it great?"

And he left me with proof that it is: "I was with [Mexican] President Fox last night for several hours," Chambers said. "He clearly gets it."

CHAPTER FOUR

BILL GATES

The Alpha Nerd and His Alter Egos

It was getting unbearable to be Bill Gates.

He was, for starters, hating his job. The company he had founded and built into a colossus was taking a beating from federal antitrust lawyers. He had too much to worry about—legal, administrative, political—none of it fun. Chief among his frustrations was that he was getting to spend little time on the technology work he loved most.

During one meeting, Gates's voice broke and his eyes teared up. Over the next several months, his colleagues at Microsoft noticed that Gates was becoming increasingly overwrought, distracted, quicker tempered. They worried about his mental health. He seemed to be losing weight and sleep.

At a particularly low moment of the antitrust trial, Gates even contemplated leaving Microsoft. Not seriously, and never publicly. But things were bad enough that he mentioned the possibility to Steve Ballmer, his closest friend and longtime deputy. "Just to blow off steam," Gates recalled to me in his office several months later. "Hey, if they really screw the company that badly," he said to Ballmer, "really just split it up in a totally irrational way. . . ."

As he said this, Ballmer, who was sitting a few feet away, stared at his feet.

"You know," Gates continued, "would it even make sense for us to, you know." He paused. "At least mentally there was that one point. . . ."

He doesn't complete the thought.

That Gates could even consider such a measure was a signal that the World's Richest Man needed a life's rewiring. So early in 2000, Gates, with the blessing and urging of his board, gave himself a present. He restored himself to full-time nerd status, stepping down as chief executive of Microsoft and assuming the title of chief software architect. He would remain as chairman of the company he had founded 25 years earlier. The rest he would leave to Ballmer.

On January 13, the day the switch was to be announced, Gates called a few friends in advance to tell them.

"Well, Steve certainly got the short end of that stick," longtime Microsoft executive Nathan Myhrvold told Gates.

"I know, he really did," Gates said, laughing. "Thank God he's willing to do this for me."

Steve Ballmer would do anything for Bill Gates. Same with Gates for Ballmer. Although the two men were assuming new roles, the company's intellectual and emotional center would remain where it always had: in the complex and symbiotic relationship between Gates and Ballmer, corporate America's most powerful buddy act—or bully act, depending on one's perspective. To understand the bond between them is to understand why Microsoft has become the exemplar of New-Economy dominance—and America's most embattled company.

It's also key to understanding Bill Gates. He is the marquee tycoon of this era, thus seemingly familiar and known. But for as central as he's been to the global economy—and for as closely watched as he is—Gates remains a scantily known figure. Over the years, I've been in several interviews with Gates, both alone and in groups, and it is always immediately clear that his popular image—the cranky–genius–gazillionaire-with-greasy-hair Gates— relays nowhere near the full-measure of the man's peculiarities. Perhaps more than any other person I've come to know, Gates projects a recurring and palpable sense of, simply, not being like the rest of us.

On the most superficial level, he looks and sounds different. There's a perpetual adolescent quality to his appearance—with his round head, mop of light brown hair, and floppy posture that make him look like a bespectacled Muppet. He has a high and squeally voice that cracks a lot, especially when he's agitated. He has a pale, oily face that, in recent years, has taken on a jowliness that makes him look more adult than he used to, but still not fully mature. He is a lousy shaver, with small black patches of stubble sprouting from his pasty face, especially on his chin.

Gates rocks vigorously when he is sitting, a trademark habit that dates to his toddler days and, for whatever reason, is a common trait among math, science, and computer genius types— including Ballmer, though not so often or in a way that's so pronounced as Gates. When rocking, Gates tucks his elbows into his thighs and brings his chin down almost to his kneecaps, then back up again. When he's thinking hard, he rocks faster; slower when he is relaxed. You almost never see Gates sit still.

Certain famous people, and many top executives, have a been-to-finishing-school quality about them. They seem to have, or acquire, a deep voice, a courtly presence, and an easy gladhanding style. Not Gates. He has a limp handshake to match his hunched posture. I've never heard him "respectfully disagree" about any- thing. He will contest things in quick spasms of disdain. "Do you know WHAT you're talking about!?" he snapped to my colleague Steven Pearlstein at a breakfast interview here at the *Washington Post* in 1998 on a visit just before the antitrust trial was to begin. He raised his voice several times that day. He asked someone if he was "technical enough" to discuss a certain topic. One industry watcher calls him "a feral executive," referring to the unpolished, unself-conscious, and unapologetic way he will attack anything or anyone that defies his impulse, reason, or objectives.

Implicit in this assessment is that Gates is a lone-wolf type under siege, both victim and predator ensconced in the righteous maw of his intellect. But as I spent time with Gates, and talked to people who have known and watched him, it became clear that his relationship with Ballmer is part of a formative pattern throughout his life. He has always picked out an alter ego, someone to nourish less-developed sides of himself while matching his I.Q. and zeal. Gates has been willing to "outsource" large portions of his intellect and psyche to a chosen partner. Ballmer is neatly suited to that role, especially now, as Microsoft proceeds as boldly as ever, despite a federal court ruling that has declared it an illegal monopoly. Likewise, Ballmer's increasingly powerful presence as Microsoft's CEO allowed Gates to tend to himself, his image, and his company at a time when everything seemed to be crashing down around him.

A NETWORK THEMSELVES

Gates and Ballmer have been friends since they met as Harvard dorm mates twenty-six years ago. Like many high-tech pioneers, the two enjoyed comfortable suburban childhoods that whetted, rather than dulled, their drive to succeed. They embody the old-money and new-money prototypes of twentieth-century affluence: Gates is the great-grandson of the man who founded Seattle's National City Bank in 1911; Ballmer's father, a Swiss immigrant who settled his family in the Detroit suburb of Farmington Hills, was a Ford Motor Co. accountant who began trumpeting his expectation that his son would attend Harvard when the boy was 8.

Both endured early social problems that friends say marked them for life. Ballmer was so shy that he would hyperventilate before going to Hebrew school. "I was just so scared," he told me. "So I wouldn't throw up, my mom would have to make me take short breaths." Today, his motivational speeches at Microsoft events are legend, but before he gets to the part where he runs through high-fiving, cheering crowds till he doubles over, sweating and panting, he has to psych himself into the idea that he's up to the performance.

William Henry Gates III (nicknamed "Trey," card-playing slang for a three) was a boy prodigy born into a wealthy Seattle family. His father, William II, was a prominent corporate lawyer; his mother, Mary, was active in local charities and was head of the local United Way chapter. Bill, the middle of three children, had older and younger sisters, Kristiane and Libby. When his mother called to him over the intercom and asked what he was doing in his room, Bill would ignore her. Finally, recalled one friend, he would shout "I'm thinking" in the direction of the intercom.

Bill was maniacally curious, emotionally raw, and often defiant. "The Gateses didn't know what to do with Trey," said the Reverend Marvin Evans, the father of Gates's best friend in adolescence. They sent him to a child psychiatrist, where he spent many of his youthful hours. He was small for his age, and endured teasing and roughhousing from his peers.

He found solace in computers, which became the object of a full-on obsession shortly after he discovered them at age 12. Like Gates, many brilliant computing leaders started out as outcasts, said Christine Comaford, a Gates friend who worked at Microsoft in the 1980s. "When they find a world that embraces them, they tend to swing the other way," Comaford said. They become hyperaggressive and driven. "They find their path to success and they'll do anything not to turn back."

As Gates and Ballmer grew to adulthood, they passed through a New-Economy version of an old boys' network. At the exclusive Lakeside School in Seattle in the late 1960s, Gates met not only his best friend, Kent Evans, but also his Microsoft co-founder, Paul Allen. Gates met Ballmer at Harvard, which they attended with future Sun Microsystems founder Scott McNealy and Excite@Home CEO George Bell.

In building Microsoft, however, Gates and Ballmer became a network unto themselves. They are stylistic opposites, both open to caricature: Gates, with smeared glasses and perfect scores on five high school achievement tests, is the petulant nerd. Ballmer, 6 feet 1, 225 pounds, and bald, speaks in a rollicking bullhorn voice—his vocal cords once required surgical repair from excessive shouting-and is the corporate evangelist.

Beyond the caricatures, both men are repeatedly called the two smartest people at Microsoft. Their intelligence is often described in computing terms, the semantic wont of many techie types. "Steve is a Pentium in a land of 386s," said former Microsoft executive Jon Roberts. "Bill is also a Pentium. But they have different optimizations. Steve is the graphic engine, smarter in an extroverted way. Bill does logic computation thinking better. He can look at a spreadsheet and immediately hone in on a question about marketshare in Spain. His level of penetration is extreme."

Gates and Ballmer are both called loyal, impatient, tenacious, and insecure, qualities reflected in a corporate culture marked by devotion, self-flagellation, and a searing suspicion of the non-Microsoft world. Some people wonder whether Ballmer amplifies Gates's natural ruthlessness—to the point where it has contributed to the company's antitrust problems.

"Steve and Bill are complementary personalities that are more likely to inflame than temper each other," said Bob Metcalfe, the founder of 3Com, who has known both men for several years. "There are three monopolies in high tech—Cisco, Intel, and Microsoft—and only one has an antitrust problem," he said. "They have failed to internalize that they're the world's most valuable company." Gates and Ballmer "are like huge teenage boys who don't know how big they've gotten, and they keep knocking things over."

Other powerful duos have led high-tech companies, but few, if any, have been so enduring. Apple co-founders Steve Jobs and Steve Wozniak (and later, Jobs and CEO John Scully) had periods of strain, if not alienation. So did AOL co-founders Steve Case and Jim Kimsey, Netscape's Jim Clark and Marc Andreessen, and Oracle's Larry Ellison and Bob Miner. Gates and Paul Allen also grew apart as Microsoft grew huge.

If Gates comes to trust someone enough, a former Microsoft executive says, he's willing to enter into a "mind-meld" relationship, an entity that doubles his capacity for thought and stokes his voracious ambition.

Early in his life, that person was Kent Evans, the most profound influence on Gates in his youth. In his late adolescence and early adulthood, it was Paul Allen.

As Microsoft rose to dominance, Gates found Steve Ballmer.

"EXPLORATION"

It can be maddening to converse with both men at the same time. One giggles when the other talks, even when no humor is apparent. They speak over each other. Or they communicate in clauses, their understanding too rapid for sentences. "Someone will have to say, 'Can you repeat that for me? I didn't quite get it,'" Microsoft executive Mich Mathews said.

This rang true when I interviewed Gates and Ballmer together in December 2000 for a *Washington Post* story I was working on about their partnership. I found the men sitting together in Gates's office in Building 8 of Microsoft's campus in

Redmond, Washington. The office had no special view and no more space than a typical Holiday Inn room. Gates's desk was surrounded by framed pictures—wife Melinda, 5-year-old daughter, 2-year-old son, and Microsoft's first eleven employees. There was a framed black-and-white photo of Einstein and three framed *Economist* magazine covers, which Gates said carry no significance whatsoever except that his sister got them for him and he's a tough person to buy gifts for and it just seemed like a good place to put the things.

Seated in a chair in the middle of the room, Gates was rocking slowly when I walked in, grinning over something, looking notably unembattled. Ballmer was the one sitting on the couch with his head in his hands. It was 9:15 A.M., and the CEO was on his third meeting of the day—fourth if you include the working game of pickup basketball he plays every Wednesday. He rubbed his hands over his crimson cheeks when I walked in, as if to revive himself.

At one point in an hour-long interview, Gates and Ballmer were discussing their aforementioned head-of-state phenomenon. The conversation went like this:

BALLMER: If you have a president of a country—

GATES: Head of state—

BALLMER: A head of state here, some heads of state will just meet with me because I'm the CEO, but you know, the head of state's a head of state and I don't care if it's a small state.

GATES, laughing: Don't think we have a lot of, you know— it's not like, you know—

BALLMER: It's not like Putin has been into town lately or something. But you know, the president of Costa Rica's been here, or Chile—

GATES: Chile or Poland—

BALLMER: Poland, you know.

GATES: That was last month.

ME: Do you guys divide up countries or something?

GATES: No, no, I get—

BALLMER: In some ways—

GATES: I get the head of state of countries—

BALLMER: Mauritius I was able to handle on my own.

GATES: I was worried about it, though.

While Gates and Ballmer's conversations are fluid, their words can be acidic; if they disagree, they can't help but bicker, and the fervor of their discourse sets the tone for Microsoft's fiercely combative culture. "We come from a philosophy where there's generally a right answer and a wrong answer," Gates said. "And if you explore it enough, everybody will just agree there's a right answer and a wrong answer."

"Exploration" at Microsoft often occurs at high volume. "It can be a knife fight," said Vern Raburn, a former Microsoft executive. "It would appear to many people that it's getting personal. Bill will always say, 'That's the stupidest thing I've ever heard.'" (The more accurate and common wording: "That's the stupidest *fucking* thing I've ever heard.")

"This is not a place to come for high stroking," said Ballmer, who can give as well as he gets, and which is central to his ability to coexist with Gates. "Steve has found a way to work with Bill without subjugating himself," Raburn said. "The moment you subjugate yourself to Bill, it can get a little dangerous. . . . He can be an alpha male in collaborative situations in ways I don't know if he realizes."

While he and Ballmer are similar in elemental ways, Gates can appreciate that Ballmer has a radically different style, personality, and outlook, all of which can be useful to him and to Microsoft. The distinctions abound.

Gates loves bridge; Ballmer loves basketball. Gates nibbles at French fries; Ballmer eats muffins by ripping the tops off and shoving them into his mouth. At a toast during Gates's bachelor party weekend in Las Vegas in late 1993, Ballmer, his best man, teased his friend as "someone who sees life as complex," rife with shades of gray. "NOT ME," he boomed. "WITH ME, IT'S BLACK OR WHITE, ON OR OFF."

"It would be great to see the world in such a black and white way," Gates said mockingly. "It would be much simpler." A long discussion about philosophical approaches to the world ensued among the twenty people who were present. This apparently is what Bill Gates and his pals do at bachelor parties.

Gates is a nearly mystical figure at Microsoft. Ballmer is frontally engaged. Gates breathes Microsoft. Ballmer exhales it.

On a hot day in June 2000, Microsoft celebrated its twenty-fifth birthday at Seattle's Safeco Field, an all-hands bash at which Ballmer popped out of a giant cake, raced through the crowd to Kool and the Gang's "Celebration," panting, sweating, gyrating, soaking a black polo shirt. He then jumped up on a stage and screamed a favorite story about how he was once addressing customers in Colombia and was playfully throwing baseballs into the crowd when one of them smacked a customer in the head. The man lost consciousness and Ballmer rushed to his side. "I begged, I pleaded," Ballmer screamed, recounting the incident televangelist-like, sweat pouring off his knobby bald head. "Bring that customer to life." The customer revived. Ballmer gave him a copy of Microsoft Office. "And from the ashes he rose up again," Ballmer wailed. "And to this day, this is the most important thing that ever happened in Colombia in IT."

Microsoft's employees stood and applauded. Ballmer raised his arms, looking triumphant, if not quite dignified.

And Gates was safe backstage, happy to outsource such motivational indignity to his best friend.

Ballmer, whose father toiled thirty years at Ford, takes an old economy view of corporate loyalty. Executives who leave Microsoft dread telling Ballmer. "He takes it very personally," said one who left in January 2000. "You expect these meetings to be emotional." When this executive told Ballmer he would be leaving, Ballmer seemed stricken. After a discussion about the executive's new job, the discussion turned to Ballmer's father, who had just died. This executive's father had died two years before. Ballmer closed the door of his office, and the two men shared a cry and a discussion about their fathers, ending with a bearhug.

Gates hates being touched. At a Microsoft event that featured Shaquille O'Neal, Gates became visibly agitated when, to the crowd's delight, the 7-foot basketball star wrapped his arms around the 5-foot-9 Gates and lifted him up.

"Bill gives off a physical reaction that says, 'Step back a little bit,'" said Christine Comaford. When he used to fly commercial, Gates sat with a blanket covering his head so he could sleep and also not be recognized. One former Microsoft executive recalls walking through the Tokyo Airport with Gates in 1996. Gates instructed the executive to appear as if they were locked in an intense conversation, so celebrity-gawkers would be less likely to approach. At the luggage rack, when the executive turned away for a moment to retrieve his bag, a man walked up to Gates claiming they'd met at a party. "Bill had this really tired, beleaguered look on his face," the executive recalled.

Gates communicates largely by e-mail. Whenever I've written to him, his responses were always prompt, always thoughtful, and often went on for several pages. He would answer my specific questions, yet the e-mails were always completely impersonal. Not that I'd expect them to be chummy, or even familiar. But there was never so much as a greeting at the top, never a "hi," and certainly never any use of my name—all of which is consistent with Gates's typical e-mail mode with his closest friends. In one note to me, Gates simply began with "Sorry it took me a few days to write down my thoughts on these questions—here they are" and he proceeded. He never signed his e-mails when he was done; he just finished writing and stopped. It was the e-mail equivalent of not touching.

Ballmer is a fat-fingered and erratic e-mailer ("graet tnx"). He prefers to invade personal space and pop his head into offices—and he often startles people.

When Microsoft executives want face-time with Ballmer, they call his executive assistant, Debby Hill, to find out where his meetings are that day so they can walk or ride the campus shuttle with him.

Gates is more likely to dispatch with an unscheduled meeting by saying "Send me mail [e-mail] on that" or "Aren't we supposed to have a meeting on that tomorrow? We'll talk about it then."

Ballmer is the prime minister. Gates is the king—and you don't touch the king. "Steve is a guy you want to be loyal to," Comaford says. "Bill is more of a guy to be in awe of."

Ballmer has been called the company's id. In the late 1980s, acting on a challenge from another executive, he stripped to his white boxers and swam across Lake Bill, an artificial lake at the center of Microsoft's campus.

When called upon, he'll also play bad cop. "Bill can be a complete wimp," Myhrvold said. "There was one very big acquisition deal where Bill says to me, 'Now, don't let me get alone with this guy, because I'll just agree.'" Myhrvold adds that Ballmer doesn't relish playing the tough guy, and if he offends someone, he often acts "like a Saint Bernard puppy who knocks you over and then starts licking your face."

He is also prone to mood swings. "We're golden, we're golden," Ballmer will say in an up moment, and "We're fucked, we're fucked," during the inevitable swoon. Gates wallows in grays, harps on problems, "tastes every drop of misery," a Microsoft executive said. "If I'm worried about something at work," Gates said, "it's there twenty-four hours a day."

In September 1996, Gates made a presentation at San Francisco's Moscone Center to announce the launch of its latest version of Internet Explorer. Afterward, he took some engineers and executives to the hotel bar next door to celebrate.

But Gates, drinking white Russians, fixated on a Microsoft e-mail product and started working himself up about "what a piece of sh—" it was. His tablemates had nothing to do with the product and prodded Gates. "Yeah," Gates said, "that's the worst piece of software we've ever shipped," and he ranted for about twenty minutes.

Ballmer was not pleased with the answers at a 1998 meeting with seven managers who worked on Microsoft Office. "Does anyone here understand Office?" he yelled, according to someone who was being yelled at. He jumped up from a conference table in Building 18, his shirt coming untucked in the back. "Anyone?" He told a nearby secretary to "get someone on the phone who understands Office."

Ballmer and Gates's relationship is commonly called a "marriage," even by the principals. "We trusted each other from the very beginning in a very deep way," Gates said. It is a hallmark of their relationship that they treat each other as roughly as they treat others. They sit next to each other in meetings, giggle, and yell—"and no one likes to see mom and dad fight," said Mich Mathews.

But they'll usually make up quickly. Microsoft executive Deborah Willingham recalled a meeting shortly after the release of Windows 95. Excess software was accumulating in stores. Ballmer took responsibility, but Gates wouldn't let the issue die.

"Why do we do this?" he said.

"Look, I said I made that mistake," Ballmer thundered to the man his children call Uncle Bill. "How many times do you want to hear me say I made that mistake?"

"Well," Gates said, smiling, "I might want to hear it a few more times."

NOTES IN THE MARGINS

Whenever I watch Gates up close, particularly in question-and-answer settings, I'm reminded of the sheer volume of things that the leader of Microsoft needs to be an expert on: technical matters of great diversity and detail; the nuances of U.S. antitrust law; the administrative challenges of running a huge and growing company; the diplomatic stresses of managing numerous corporate partnerships; the financial arcana that Wall Street is concerned with. And then there are the matters intrinsic to being Gates, the scrutiny that goes with being the richest man in the world, and one of the most controversial.

As a practical matter, I've always wondered how Gates stays abreast of the things he needs to stay abreast of. I asked him about his reading diet. Each morning, he told me, he reads the *Wall Street Journal,* usually on paper, and the online version of the *New York Times.* He will also visit a bunch of news and technology Web sites such as CNET.com, Zdnet, MSNBC. None of this is unusual for a well-informed technology executive. What is, however, are the libraries of books, research papers, trade journals, and, basically, everything, that Gates will read with tremendous speed and apparent comprehension. He has seamless recall of the most obscure articles, software parameters, arcane laws. By the age of 9, Gates had read the *World Book Encyclopedia* from A to Z, according to *Gates,* a biography by Stephen Manes and Paul Andrews.

Gates brings thirty books with him on a typical vacation, he tells me. He will read "more than a book a day" on a pleasure trip and usually gets through most of them. He will also set aside two "Think Weeks" a year in which he will hole up somewhere and bore through several dozen books as well as research papers, memos, articles, and anything else that piles up on one of his numerous "to read" piles. He will scribble notes, comments, and critiques in the margins of the books he reads, and will often send his marked-up books to the author.

Gates says he is a "pretty fast reader," though not a trained speed-reader. When he was young, he had a friend who took an Evelyn Woods course, and they would compete over who could read something faster. "My reading is very variable," Gates said. "It just depends on the material that I'm reading. If it's something about math, my view is, you just reread the page to make sure that you get everything." He said science books also take him longer; so do books about his beloved pastime, bridge, because he takes the time to envision the models in his head. "There's this book, *How the Mind Works*, which is a [Steven] Pinker book," Gates said. "I spent twenty hours reading that book because I was writing so many notes in the margin."

None of Gates's reading would be classified as light, at least by most people. When I was in the Seattle office of Patty Stonesifer, a former Microsoft executive who is now head of Gates's $23.5-billion foundation, she had just received an e-mail from Gates in which he summarized and critiqued everything he had read on a just-concluded vacation. These were long and detailed accounts that went on for several pages, things he often sends to select friends, especially when his reading relates to an area of interest that they have in common. He had just read several books, papers, and journals about world health issues, the focal point of his foundation, and he was thus downloading his findings to Stonesifer.

She would not share the contents of Gates's e-mail, but she did
read me a sampling of his reading choices: "Consensus Statement
on Antiretroviral Treatment for AIDS in Poor Countries" from individual members of Harvard University's faculty; *Child Nutrition
and the Wealth of Nations* by Reynaldo Martorell; *Combination
Therapy for Malaria in Africa: Hype or Hope?* by Peter Bloland, et
al., from the Bulletin of the World Health Organization, *The
Evidence Base for Interventions to Prevent HIV Infection in Low
and Middle Income Countries—The World Health Organization's
Commission on Macroeconomics and Health; Critical Issues in
Global Health* edited by C. Everett Koop; *The Invisible Enemy: A
Natural History of Viruses* by Dorothy Crawford; and *Infections
and Inequalities: The Modern Plagues* by Paul Farmer.

And several others.

Stonesifer reminded me that this was just one Gates vacation,
in one area of interest. There were other sets of e-mails that he sent
to select parties in other topics he cares about, such as software
design. And in a given week, Gates will also *write* the equivalent of
a book in e-mail, dozens of them every day in which he unfurls
ideas and criticisms to an extended kitchen cabinet of friends, colleagues, and random people he hears about and who interest him
and who he can get in touch with because he is, after all, Bill Gates.

Gates is a full-contact intellect. He seeks out partners to
scheme and explore with, and bash against. He handpicks the
most elite ones he can find and occasionally, thrice in his life, he
will find a super-partner who recasts his notion of what's possible
and what he can accomplish. It started when he was 12.

NERDS TOGETHER

Kent Hood Evans was Gates's boyhood best friend. He was
dreamy, dogged, and largely devoid of inhibition. He carried

Barron's and *Fortune* around Lakeside School in his enormous briefcase. Until he met Kent, Gates had never shown any interest in business or even making money.

Like Gates, Evans was brilliant and precocious; unlike Gates, he was extremely directed. In a résumé for a summer job, he once wrote: "I am looking for a job that involves programming that I consider interesting." He pushed Gates to think big and take risks, and Gates would marvel at his friend's nerve. Kent often tried to convince him to skip school and join him at a computing center across town, but more often than not, Gates was afraid of getting caught. Kent, he recalled, was fearless, and after a while, Gates also learned to be fearless.

Evans loved politics and government. He wrote frequent letters to public officials, typing with a distinctive two-finger style in which his left pointer controlled the shift key and his right pointer mashed down loudly on the letters. He volunteered for several hours a week on Hubert Humphrey's presidential campaign and once asked Gates if he would be interested in joining him in a foreign service career. Maybe, he said, it could result in an ambassadorship one day. "This is, like, ninth grade," Gates said.

They were both distinctive: Gates was slight and unkempt with pants pulled up way too high; Kent was heavyset and born with a cleft palate. They were nerds together, showing no discernible interest in girls, music, or any other teen-boy passions— although Kent was one of the most popular boys in his Lakeside class. Gates, who was unrestrained in railing about peers and teachers he considered stupid, was not. He was "an extremely annoying person," one Lakeside classmate told Manes and Andrews in *Gates*. "He was very easy to sort of dislike. And I think that probably me and a lot of people took a little extra pleasure in sort of bumping him while passing him in the hall. . . . In public school, the guy would've been killed."

Gates and Evans would speak for hours on the phone at night, sharing ideas about business and computers. They recommended books to each other, argued, developed a deep understanding of their subject, and communicated in a kind of shorthand. At Microsoft, Gates would call this "high-bandwidth communication."

In the late 1960s, Lakeside was one of the first schools in the country to have a computer. Housed in a small room in McAlister Hall, it was a Teletype machine about the size of a microwave oven that became a magnet for math whizzes Gates and Evans, and upperclassmen Paul Allen and Ric Weiland, who would become among Microsoft's first employees. They formed the Lakeside Programmers Group, not "club," because "club" connoted a hobbyist's pursuit with all its attendant frivolity. It was called a "group" because that sounded more businesslike and their goal was to make money.

The group operated with minimal supervision. This was by design, said Fred Wright, the Lakeside math chairman, who provided that supervision. "Our philosophy was, get a group of smart people together, give them tools, and get out of the way," Wright said. That, he says, is the best environment to spur creativity, competition, and collaboration. It can foster dynamic collisons and ideas between personalities at a defining stage of life. "If you want to see the roots of Microsoft's culture, look no further than the Lakeside Programmers Group," Kent's father said.

The four boys spent late-night hours at Seattle's Computer Center Corp. ("C-cubed"), which offered time on a Digital Equipment Corp. machine per an agreement with Lakeside. When C-cubed went out of business in 1970, the Lakeside Programmers Group nearly imploded in civil war. Gates and Evans—without the knowledge of their partners—arranged to buy a set of DEC tapes cheap in a bankruptcy auction. They hid the tapes in a room at Lakeside, and when Allen learned of this, he found and kept them. Livid, Gates and Evans threatened legal action.

They were 15.

At one point, the older kids—Allen and Weiland—told Gates and Evans that they weren't needed on a particular project. But when Allen and Weiland became overworked, they invited Evans and Gates back. Gates agreed to return, but on one condition: He needed to be in charge of the project.

Bill and Kent were inseparable and overextended. School and computers ate up most of their time, the latter more so as they took on consulting jobs, often in exchange for computing time. In their junior year, 1971–1972, a Lakeside teacher enlisted them to automate the school's complex class-scheduling system. They pulled a string of all-nighters, hoping to have the program ready for their senior year. Evans took a break to go mountain climbing over the Memorial Day weekend. He slipped and fell to his death on May 28, 1972, in an accident his father attributes to the fatigue caused by his loaded schedule.

"Kent's death was a huge loss to Bill," Paul Allen recalled. Gates was scheduled to speak at Kent's funeral, but he was too distraught and sobbed through the service. "Having your best friend die really makes you step back and think about life quite a bit," Gates recalled in an e-mail. "I was devastated." When Marvin Evans met Melinda Gates a few years ago, she said her husband still talked about Kent all the time.

"It's been nearly thirty years," Gates said, "and I still remember his phone number."

A BASIC MISSION

Even in his grief, Gates was determined to finish the Lakeside scheduling project. In choosing a new collaborator, he turned to Paul Allen. Allen was enrolled at Washington State University, but agreed to help when he returned home for the summer. They completed their work for Lakeside and held out the possibility of doing other projects together.

Gates headed east to Harvard in 1973, where he told friends that he was eager to be among an elite group of students who could challenge him intellectually.

In his sophomore year, a mutual friend, Jeff Clark, introduced Gates to Ballmer. "Jeff liked Steve because Steve had this very energetic approach to being involved in everything," Gates said with a sniffly laugh. "And he kind of liked me because I had this very energetic approach to not being involved in things."

They both lived in Currier House, an outpost full of math and science whizzes removed from the more centrally located Harvard dorms along the Charles River. "In return for living farther away, the male–female ratio was better," Gates said. "And you could have a hamburger at every meal." Ballmer said he availed himself to neither the favorable male–female ratio nor to the hamburgers. Gates said he ate a lot of hamburgers.

Ballmer compensated for his shyness by becoming hyperactive on campus. He would become the manager of the Harvard football team, business manager of the *Harvard Crimson,* and publisher of a campus literary magazine. He made a point of memorizing faces and names from the Harvard directory.

He and Gates became friends, attending a double feature of *Singing in the Rain* and *A Clockwork Orange* that November. The next month, Gates left the door to his dorm room wide open when he returned to Seattle for the holidays; because dorm mates hung out in Gates's room, he never locked the door. Ballmer, seeing his friend's wallet sitting in full view on his dresser, locked up after him.

Both got perfect scores on their math SATs, shared an interest in Napoleon, and were both lousy at hiding their bad moods. They were both horrific slobs. Gates eschewed sheets, opting to sleep directly on his mattress because it was too much trouble to make his bed. Gary Kollin, who briefly shared an apartment with

Ballmer one summer, said Ballmer did the same. His sheets were the wrong size for his mattress, and he thought it would be a waste of money to buy new ones for the summer. Once, Kollin recalled, Ballmer left a watermelon rind out on the kitchen counter for a week, a particularly hot week, and it created the lingering aroma of rotting watermelon in the apartment that summer.

Gates was memorably hygiene-challenged, his dorm mates said. He had a distinctive odor—mingling perspiration, unwashed clothes, and hallitosis—that former dorm mates still recall vividly as "the Bill smell." "We'd have these poker games, and I would always look to see where Bill was sitting, then sit as far away as possible," recalls Scott Drill, a friend from Currier House. "He certainly didn't seem to be showering very much."

Ballmer nudged Gates into doing social things, if not into showering more. Ballmer persuaded him to join Harvard's all-male Fox Club. But each had his own interests and circles, and Gates's social life revolved mainly around playing poker with dorm mates in the Currier House basement. The poker games went all night, the most popular being seven-card high-low, with some of the bigger wins getting as high as $500 or $600.

The games often went badly for Gates. "We used to rub our hands together when he'd sit down," Drill said. "We'd say, 'Here comes the Bill Gates Gravy Train.'" Gates had a locked-in willingness to keep playing, even after his losses shot up into the hundreds. He was always good about writing checks to promptly settle his losses. After one particularly bad run, he walked into Ballmer's room and handed him his checkbook. "Hide this," he instructed Ballmer. "I don't want to lose anymore."

Neither Gates nor Ballmer required much sleep, and friends recall them debating loudly late into the night, both of them rocking together in unconscious unison. One of their disagreements was over how they could best "make a difference" in the world after they left Harvard. Gates spoke of returning to Seattle to be

162 BILL GATES   The Alpha Nerd and His Alter Egos

closer to his family, which Ballmer dismissed on the grounds that
he (Gates) needed to go to a bigger city to prove himself. Ballmer
was considering government, which Gates thought was foolish.
He talked about going into business.

They studied together until dawn several days in a row for an
economics final. "We're fucked in this class. . . . No, we're
golden," Ballmer would yell late at night. Gates scored a 99 on the
test; Ballmer, a 97.

Gates's friendship with Ballmer developed in parallel with
Gates and Allen's computer work, which continued as Allen
moved to Boston and took a job at Honeywell Corp. Whereas
Gates and Ballmer forged their union over classwork, mutual
friends, and typical collegiate angst, Gates and Allen bonded
wholly over computers.

Allen was like Kent Evans in that he spurred—and reinforced—big ideas in Gates. Gates was already sold on the magic of
computing and the challenge of making money from it. At Lakeside,
friends recall him predicting—not fantasizing—that he would be a
millionaire by the time he turned 30. But Allen was the one who
convinced Gates that computers would one day, and soon, become
accessible to mass markets, not just businesses and government enti-
ties such as schools. Chips were growing exponentially in speed and
power, and it was just a question of someone developing the right
hardware. They needed to position their goals accordingly.

"We became best friends dreaming about what we could do
when our best software ideas combined with chip magic," Gates
said of he and Allen in an e-mail. In Gates's trilogy of alter-egos,
Allen was the one who stoked and directed his sense of techno-
logical possibility. The extroverted Evans and Ballmer thought like
businessmen. Allen, too, to a point, but he was foremost a brilliant technologist, and also a dreamer. Without Allen's impetus,
Gates would have likely floated along brilliantly but unfocused,
another red-eyed nerd in the computing center. Allen got him to

take a leap of faith that a not-yet-invented tool would come along sooner than anyone expected—and that it was worth their efforts to assume that it would.

In late 1974, Allen was walking through Harvard Square when his leap of faith was rewarded at "The Out of Town" newsstand. He was stopped in his sneakers by the January 1975 issue of *Popular Electronics*. The cover bore a picture of a boxy machine with toggle switches called the Altair 8080.

The world's first personal computer.

Allen bought the magazine and raced to Currier House. He and Gates wrote a letter to MITS, the Albuquerque-based maker of the Altair, and offered to write software for the machine in BASIC, the popular programming language. The people at MITS said go ahead, but warned that the *Popular Electronics* article had won them a great deal of attention, and a lot of people were offering to write software for their machine.

Gates's and Allen's lives were suddenly boiled down to a mission: to develop software for the Altair in BASIC. Soon Allen moved to Albuquerque; Gates dropped out of Harvard in his junior year to follow him in 1975. They formed a consultancy called Micro-Soft.

In their rush to write BASIC for the Altair, Gates and Allen enlisted the help of a Currier House resident named Monte Davidoff to write an intricate but crucial part of the software. Davidoff, a shy, middle-class kid from Glendale, Wisconsin, was charged with writing a portion of the software that would allow the Altair to perform a greater range of calculations. He developed the "floating point" math package for the software that allowed the Altair to read numbers with no fixed decimal point. Gates and Allen were focused on other things, and were happy to leave this to Davidoff.

Davidoff's experience offers a glimpse at the fine line between fame and footnote in computing history. It is also a window into Bill Gates's collaborative style when he is dealing with a more timid personality, someone he viewed as an unequal partner. Davidoff was a "sweet, unassuming, really quiet guy," recalled Gary Kollin. "He was the kind of guy Bill Gates would walk all over."

In Albuquerque, Davidoff lived with Gates and Allen in a two-bedroom apartment, sleeping on the living room floor. They became friends, Davidoff says, but Gates rode him hard. "There was definitely a supervisory dynamic," Davidoff says. "Bill could get very loud. If he felt you weren't getting something, he would say the same thing, louder. . . . He liked strong interchanges. I preferred not to work in that way."

Davidoff spent the summers of 1975 and 1977 working for Gates and Allen in Albuquerque. They offered him a permanent job with Microsoft (the hyphen was eliminated in 1976). Davidoff, whose father co-owned a small Milwaukee hardware store, said no, chiefly because he didn't want to drop out of Harvard. Gates, with family money in reserve, could afford to. It's a reminder that the most successful entrepreneurs are inevitably risk-takers—and it's easier to be a risk-taker if failure does not equate to starvation.

"The way Bill and I thought about money was very different," Davidoff said. "He would tell all of his friends, 'Just call me collect.' He knew he wasn't going to have to support himself coming out of college. Bill Gates is a rich-to-riches story."

Davidoff graduated from Harvard and went on to a career as a programmer. Now 45, he lives in Cupertino, California, where he works as an independent software consultant and pays the astronomical rents of Silicon Valley. He often wonders "what if," but said he's comfortable with his limited role in Microsoft's precorporate history.

He has not seen Gates for twenty-four years, except for two random encounters at industry events in San Jose.

"Monte," he recalled Gates saying when he saw him, "we wondered what ever happened to you."

DIRTY WORK

From the time he dropped out of Harvard, Gates kept track of Ballmer. They spoke by phone, and Ballmer once visited Albuquerque. After he graduated from Harvard with a degree in applied math and economics, Ballmer went to work at Procter & Gamble, where he learned how to market Coldsnap Freezer Dessert Makers and, later, Duncan Hines cake mixes.

"Steve was extremely intense, very personable, and probably the smartest man I've ever met," said Gordon Tucker, who worked with Ballmer at P&G. None of Ballmer's P&G colleagues describe him as shy, but Ballmer says he continued to battle shyness. When he grew tired of selling cake mixes, he wanted to try his hand at screenwriting. But he was petrified to tell his P&G boss he was leaving. To work up his nerve, he rolled down the windows of his blue Mustang and turned Rod Stewart's "Do You Think I'm Sexy?" up to the radio's full volume.

At Stanford Business School—his next stop after a brief stay in Hollywood—Ballmer would perform similar rituals en route to class. "He would keep telling himself, 'I'm gonna kick some ass in class today,'" said classmate Dan Rudolph, who rode with him. The sound track for this mantra was often Michael Jackson's "Rock With You."

Unlike Harvard and other East Coast business schools, Stanford placed a heavy emphasis on cooperation and teamwork. Ballmer was well liked at Stanford, but his manic style of engagement and competition played badly with some. So did his habit of advertising all the prestigious consulting firms that were offering him jobs. It thus surprised some of his Stanford friends to learn that Ballmer, after only a year, was considering a job with an unknown software company in Seattle, where Microsoft had moved in 1979. Friends recall Ballmer expressing conflicting desires—between traditional paths to success and something riskier.

But Ballmer liked Gates's ambitions, plus "he has always put a great deal of value on personal relationships," said Michael Levinthal, a Stanford classmate. "Here was this guy, Bill Gates, who he clearly trusted. And when Steve trusts someone . . . he'll invest a great deal."

Even at 24, Ballmer had fashioned a business identity for himself. He had grown comfortable in important but supportive roles: As a business manager of the *Harvard Crimson*, he supported the efforts of the writers and editors. As manager of the football team, he worked behind the scenes while others played the game. He was comfortable with dirty work. "There are two ways to succeed in business," he told friends. "One is to have the big insights. The other is to take the big insights and make it happen."

At that point, in 1980, Gates needed someone who would handle the challenge of running a growing business: hiring, personnel, finances. Essentially, Gates sought someone with whom he could join in a business mind-meld to complement the mind-meld on technology issues he already had with Allen. Ballmer flew to Seattle to spend a weekend with Gates. At dinner with Ballmer and Gates' parents, Gates shared his view that personal computers would soon be everywhere—and his software would be at the forefront of the incursion. From that dinner came a marketing phrase: "A Computer on Every Desktop Running Microsoft Software."

Gates sealed Ballmer's commitment to Microsoft in a ship-to-shore phone call from his sailboat *(The Doo-Wah)* in the British Virgin Islands. He offered Ballmer a salary of $50,000 and, more important, a significant equity stake in the company—5 percent to 10 percent. This raised some ire among the tight-knit group of early Microsoft employees, many of whom held a natural bias against non-techies like Ballmer. He was employee number twenty-four.

The Gates–Ballmer marriage erupted in quarreling before the honeymoon ended. In one of Ballmer's first acts at Microsoft, he insisted that the company needed to hire seventeen people. But for all his aggressive goals, Gates could be very tight with the corporate dollar. He maintained that Microsoft never take on debt and always have enough money to operate for a year without any sales. And he was not at all convinced that Microsoft would grow fast enough to justify Ballmer's hiring.

"You're trying to bankrupt me," Gates accused Ballmer.

The eventual resolution of the argument would foreshadow how decisions have been made at Microsoft over the years. Gates and Ballmer, after expressing their viewpoints at high volumes, eventually gnashed their dispute to a natural compromise: Ballmer could hire new employees, but he must adhere to an exceedingly rigorous hiring standard—which would include pop quizzes and brain teasers in interviews that would be widely copied among computing firms. This would ensure that Microsoft would be home to, in Gates's lexicon, "super-smart" people with "incredible processing power." As a logistical matter, it would make it almost impossible to hire as many people as fast as Ballmer wanted to.

Gates and Ballmer had another tense row early on. Because of the significant equity in Ballmer's pay package, he bore a huge and immediate tax liability—$500,000. "We didn't understand that there was a tax effect," Gates said, and it was unclear whether Ballmer or the corporation would have to pay. "I'm sitting here saying, 'Geez, I'm 24 years old . . . oh my god,'" Ballmer said.

Eventually, Gates lent Ballmer the money. Ballmer's compensation—and Gates's concern about revenue growth—were quickly mooted as Microsoft became the premier independent software company in an industry that was growing even more dramatically than Gates and Allen had imagined. Ballmer was instrumental in what would be the key business sequence in the company's early history: He helped Gates and Allen secure the purchase of the

Disk Operating System (DOS) from a small Seattle firm in 1980. DOS allowed applications software to work on personal computers, and it became the foundation for Microsoft's flagship product, MS-DOS. Ballmer then helped negotiate a landmark deal with International Business Machines to run MS-DOS on IBM's machines, as well as on millions of IBM clones.

Gates and Allen remained Microsoft's resident icons and visionaries, but as Microsoft prospered in the 1980s, Ballmer assumed an in-house status to rival theirs. And through Gates and Ballmer's frequent and heated discussions, they thrived—as if discord galvanized a deeper trust.

Gates and Allen fought a lot, too, and after a while it seemed to wear down Allen. "Working with and for Bill can be a very intense process," Allen said, chuckling. Early Microsoft employees remember that Gates and Allen would argue loudly, often over hardcore technology issues, but even over small things. One early employee recalls a "friendly" chess match between the two partners degenerating into a Gates tantrum in which he scattered the pieces on the board.

Over time, the co-founders' relationship grew strained. Allen's hours diminished, especially compared to the workaholics Gates and Ballmer. Gates and Allen stopped speaking on a few occasions. While Allen remained focused on technology, he was bored by the mounting intricacies of Microsoft's corporate life.

He began to feel ill during a trip to Europe in late 1982. He discovered a lump on his neck. He returned home to Seattle and, a few days later, was diagnosed with Hodgkin's disease. He recovered, after a grueling series of radiation treatments, but it hastened a decision to leave Microsoft, shortly after the release of DOS 2.0. This was something Allen had been contemplating before he became sick. Gates was a supportive friend to Allen during his convalescence, but not about Allen's decision to leave. "I wanted him to stay at Microsoft," Gates said. "It was that simple. And he chose, faced with his own mortality and some financial freedom . . . to have his time free."

One mutual friend said Gates was deeply wounded by Allen's decision. "Even though they grew apart, Bill had this brother's affinity for Paul. When Paul left, I think part of Bill left, and he didn't know what to do with himself. And I'm not sure Bill could ever forgive him for that."

When I asked Gates about this, he downplayed his rift with Allen and was sensitive to the impression that there ever was one. "I wouldn't say it was broken or anything," he said of their bond. He called Allen a "lifelong friend" and their partnership will be sanctified in history. At one point, Gates looked at me, almost quizzically. "Paul and I have had our dream come true like no two people," Gates said. "Everything we sat and talked about is almost sort of true."

As the years passed, Gates worked hard to repair his relationship with Allen. In 1986, the same year Microsoft's initial public offering sent the co-founders' paper fortunes soaring into the hundreds of millions, Gates and Allen gave Lakeside School $2.2 million to build a science and math center. A plaque outside the auditorium bears this dedication: "In memory of classmate, friend and fellow explorer, Kent Hood Evans."

SEMI-EXPERTS

With Allen gone, Gates came to rely even more heavily on Ballmer, whose influence quickly expanded into every quadrant as Microsoft became the epitome of high-tech supremacy.

In the 1980s, Ballmer helped oversee the team that produced the Windows operating system (engineers recall him stalking the halls at 2 A.M., clapping his hands and screaming, "Yes, yes, yes"). He built and spearheaded one of computing's most aggressive sales organizations ("Get the business, get the business"). He was Microsoft's most rabid cost watchdog ("That's big-shotty," he sniffed to an executive who had bought a cell phone in the late 1980s).

When he wanted to focus on a part of the company, he simply moved his office there—even if it was in Europe. He has bored through an intimidating level of business detail, clinging to his "yellow book," a binder in which he keeps reams of financial data on all the company's key businesses.

Gates can be "over-geeky" in his approach to product development. This is counterbalanced by Ballmer, who dumbs down discussions to incorporate the perspective of average users. In a meeting shortly before the release of Windows 2000, Ballmer posed a question to a group of engineers.

"What exactly is in here that customers are going to love?" he said. "What can I get our sales force excited about."

"Instant directory," replied Gates, who was in the meeting and seemingly dazzled by what the engineers were saying.

"Is that doo-dad actually important to people," Ballmer said, "or is it just Geek sex?"

Gates explained that the technology would allow users to see exactly who was logged onto the network at a given time. And wasn't that just so totally cool!

"Geek sex," Ballmer said, smirking, waving his hand dismissively.

In twenty years, Ballmer has held every top management job at the company. His unofficial title throughout: Bill's Number 2. Or 1.5.

As the federal antitrust trail against Microsoft began in 1998, the demands of Gates's job, which he called "inhuman" to begin with, had grown untenable. The trial added one more monstrous burden to his mental horde, and it tipped him over what he calls his "threshold."

Gates had always prided himself on his ability to compartmentalize issues without letting them bleed into one another. And he was suddenly failing that. Microsoft's engineering teams, Gates's intellectual brethren, would spend hours writing memos to him that he wouldn't have time to read or respond to. He wrote a memo to Microsoft's board in 1997 explaining his unhappiness with his job. It spurred a series of discussions that would lead to Ballmer being named president in 1998 and CEO in 2000.

When I asked Gates at what point he chose Ballmer to be his "successor" as CEO, he seemed confused. "I don't think of that word," he said. "Steve and I had worked in partnership running the company for a long, long time." Gates saw this not as any changing of the guard, but rather as a quantitative adjustment of responsibility. "I just dropped twenty, twenty-five percent of the burden," Gates said.

He made this shift in time to oversee Microsoft's .Net project. This is the company's technology initiative to develop software that will allow users and Web sites to share information and interact as seamlessly as software within a PC. It is, as Gates often says, a "bet-the-company" move, easily the most daunting technical challenge to confront Microsoft in a decade. "I am spending a lot more time with engineers, which is what I love most," he said in an e-mail.

"Our goal at Microsoft is to be successful in an incredibly tumultuous world," said Nathan Mhyrvold. "The stuff we're building now was considered impossible when we started. And we know that in eighteen months it will be passe. You try to cover that funny cusp."

No one has internalized the precariousness of computing success like Gates and Ballmer. And despite their new titles and tweaked responsibilities, Microsoft's psyche would remain steeped in the trickle-down hope and insecurity of its leaders. "Bill and Steve are two of the most confident people I know and also the most pessimistic," says one former company executive. In their extremes, he said, it can be confidence to a point of arrogance and pessimism to a point of self-loathing. "All of these things you might associate with Microsoft," he says.

When they're both in town, Gates and Ballmer meet weekly, usually for 90 minutes. It's a rare day that they don't speak or exchange e-mail. Gates tends to e-mail his ruminations throughout the weekend. Ballmer rarely does anything until Sunday night. They worry less about lines of authority than about duplicating each other's efforts.

> BALLMER: Sometimes both of us get dragged into an issue, which is stupid for us to get dragged into because—
>
> GATES: Yuh.
>
> BALLMER: —just doesn't need to take time, it should take time from one or the other but not both.
>
> GATES, laughing: Yuh. It's easier if only one of us gets dragged in. Then one of us can be the expert.
>
> BALLMER: That's the thing I talked to you about on the way home Friday night, and we're both sort of . . .
>
> GATES, laughing: Semi-experts.
>
> BALLMER: Yeah . . .

It is not clear why, but Gates keeps laughing. And Ballmer keeps nodding his head and smiling as he stares at Gates knowingly.

PUBLIC PROPERTY

"Believe me, I live the most examined life," Gates is saying six months later. The context of his statement: some of the headaches of being Bill Gates in the early twenty-first century.

"Every e-mail I've ever sent or received has been examined by multiple [agencies]. First FTC, then DOJ. So any little snippet you know that I would have said, 'Let's beat this competitor' or something, they would have brought out."

He's asked for money all the time. To the average person, wealth is what defines him—and its capitalist human nature to focus on money, not spreadsheets. It's not enough to hear a federal judge say that Microsoft behaved in a "predacious" and illegal manner, and then watch Microsoft's stock plummet by $80 billion in one day; somehow, it's more edifying, more understandable, if the plight is expressed as, "Did you know that Bill Gates lost roughly $13 billion in stock today?!"

It's difficult for Gates to go to dinner. "If I'm out at a restaurant, some type of interaction can happen," he said. "That's not uncommon." He is now public property. Myhrvold remembers sitting with Gates and watching a woman on TV speculating about his psychological well-being. She was pondering the question, "Is Bill Gates happy?"

"But I've never met her," Gates kept saying, incredulously. "How could she talk about that? How could they let her talk about that? She's never even met me."

Gates, Myhrvold said, wasn't so much angry as he was totally baffled.

It was June 11, 2001, the day Timothy McVeigh was executed, and I was sitting with Gates in his office again, this time without Ballmer. Gates was on several magazine covers that week, in anticipation of the Windows XP Operating System that was due out at year's end; and, also, a prevailing view at the time that the government's victory over Microsoft in the antitrust trial would soon be overturned on appeal—or at least sharply diminished. "The Beast Is Back" was the headline across Gates's face on that week's *Fortune*.

Gates's office was a big mess. There was a Styrofoam plate of mashed potatoes on his desk, a heaping lump covered in dark brown gravy left over from his cafeteria lunch. It was tilted at a precarious angle amid a pile of yellow legal pads, crumpled papers, a *Wall Street Journal*, a Truman biography, a balled-up sweater, and a few carrot nuggets also left over from lunch.

The desk had the feel of a college dorm room during finals week, which mirrored the disheveled and headachey way that Gates looked. He wore a dark green dress shirt (monogrammed "WHG") with large sweat spots under his arms that spread during our meeting. The shirt was untucked from the front of his slacks, his glasses were crooked, and he tapped his black loafers maniacally on the floor.

Gates was just off a conference call that ran a half-hour late. He greeted me in his office and seemed still to be very occupied in the matters discussed in the conference call. It could have been anything: the looming Court of Appeals decision; the mega-complexities of XP, Microsoft's hotly-awaited new operating system; or, the meeting he had scheduled later that day with his Gates Foundation staff to discuss prospective projects. Indeed, this or any moment's puzzle could have been anything on Gates's corner desk, a massively cluttered monument to everything he still needed to keep straight—even after outsourcing twenty percent to Ballmer.

One of my goals for this meeting was to get Gates to reflect on his reputed ordeal during the late 1990s: when he was crying in meetings, demonized by his government, attacked by seemingly everyone in high-tech, and getting pies thrown in his face by strangers in Europe. I had heard many of his friends and co-workers speak of Gates's days in the abyss of the late 1990s; "Bill's Dark Period" is what one executive called it.

But Gates wasn't playing now. He was quick to speak of how attacked he has been, how scrutinized his life was—yet he was also defiant. He had weathered the unpleasantness, had taken all that the government and his Silicon Valley antagonists had thrown at him.

And here he was, still here, rocking.

The government was not successful in vilifying him at the trial, he insisted. This is a notion that most people who followed the trial would find laughable. In fact, prosecutors made heavy use of a videotaped deposition of Gates, brooding and prickly, obfuscating over several questions. It stands as the enduring image of the landmark trial.

But Gates is talking like a man who got off easy. "They [the government] didn't even choose to call me as a witness," he said, "which they easily could have done." They used relatively few of the e-mails he had written. Gates now said he expected a positive resolution all along. "We had faith throughout that whole thing that, in the end, both the laws of encouraging innovation and Microsoft's particular role in coming out with new products, all of that would be vindicated in a very strong way."

A few weeks later, the federal appeals court ruled—and in fact it did not vindicate Microsoft in a very strong way, or at all, depending on interpretation.

The Court of Appeals reversed an earlier decision that recommended that Microsoft be broken up; and Judge Thomas Penfield Jackson, author of the earlier anti-Microsoft decision, was founded to have made inappropriately biased statements against the company in the media and was ordered off the case. But the court also upheld the ruling that Microsoft was an illegal monopoly, and the case was sent back to a new judge for a decision on what penalties would be imposed. Based on the hard line the government has taken in early settlement talks, the remedies for this could radically change how Microsoft operates in the future. As I write this, that remedy, and its effect on Microsoft, is uncertain and probably won't be resolved for months, if not years.

What was clear to me as I spoke to Gates in June, however, was that if he was infected with any resignation or humility over the trial, he was now well past it.

He was as certain and as confident as ever, contesting his place in history. "When you get this 'Hey, what's the latest in the Microsoft trial' thing," he said, "you definitely feel like, 'Hey, do people remember that the software industry was one-fiftieth of the size it is today before we came in with our model?'"

This was a different Gates than the one I met with in December, when Ballmer was with him. He seemed more isolated this time, less at ease, a little besieged. His shoulders were hunched and twitching. He kept shifting his position on his black leather couch, swaying front and back, side to side, at odd angles.

In mid-sentence, Gates simply lay down on his side, planted his left elbow on the couch and held his hand against his cheek as he continued talking.

A few minutes later, still lying on his side, he tucked his knees into his chest, almost in the fetal position. Then, a few minutes later, he stood up and switched to a seat closer to me, collapsing into the chair, rocking again.

At one point, I asked Gates if there was a burden in being so wealthy and having everyone know it. It was kind of a silly question—we should all be so burdened! Gates gave me a funny look as he took in my questions. He smiled, a little mischieveously.

"Sure," he said. "But there is an offsetting benefit."

A CONFLUENCE OF FACTORS

One of these benefits is that he gets to try to save the world. Gates spoke a great deal about his charitable work, in which he has racheted up his involvement significantly. He has given away his Microsoft stock in multibillion-dollar chunks.

That's been another consequence of Ballmer's expanded role at Microsoft: It has allowed Gates to spend more time with his foundation, which in January 2000 surpassed the Wellcome Trust of England as the largest in the world, with total assets approaching $25 billion. The Bill and Melinda Gates Foundation has made sweeping global efforts to thwart the spread of disease and increase the spread of computers. Gates has toured impoverished villages in Africa, vaccinated kids in India, and rode in a bookmobile through Alabama. And it's a funny thing, Gates said. He can get a crowd worked up into wild applause about some neat new software feature. But he was recently on a panel discussing world health issues, talking about being able to save a million lives through new research, vaccination programs, and treatment initiative—and barely anyone applauded.

"What if the foundation were dedicated to saving ten lives a year?" Gates asks. "You say, 'Hey, that's worthwhile. Ten people. I could think about that. Ten children are in the room and he's going to save all ten.'" It's not like this when it's a million lives a year. "Well, okay, that's a number on a piece of paper," Gates said. "You almost can't comprehend it."

He's had a bunch of mini-revelations like that: The basic disjointedness of how people think about things, how problems are identified, prioritized, attacked, how the world works. He gets frustrated a lot, said his foundation head Patty Stonesifer. Gates will ask her, "How are we doing on measles vaccines? How are we doing in Angola?" "It's not like I can answer with market share," she said. It's not like software, or business, a process with measurable results. This is complex, in a whole new manner of complex, and Gates can only control so much. He reads everything he can get his hands on about diarrhea, AIDS in Africa, immunization strategies, Alpha-Rice, and every so often, someone from the Gates Foundation will send over an enormous pile of research papers, articles, and books for him to read.

Lanky and spirited with reddish hair, Stonesifer is the former head of Microsoft's Interactive Division and has become something of an alter-ego to the philanthropic Gates. So have his wife,

Melinda, and his father, Bill, all of whom have sunk themselves together into the dicey scientific, cultural, political, and economic issues involved in fighting disease on a global scale. They read, discuss, meet regularly. They are a dynamic salon, just like any other dynamic salon, except that they have $23.5 billion to play with and a lot more where that came from.

Friends say that through his charitable work, Gates has become somewhat radicalized about life, the world, problem-solving. He has also become more openly emotional. He tells me about he and Melinda crying when they watch videos of kids starving around the world, or when Melinda returned home from India and told him about an AIDS hospital she visited there. In a sense, Gates's foundation work constitutes a kind of intellectual and emotional mind-meld at a new stage of his life.

On June 9, 2000, the day Judge Jackson ordered the break-up of Microsoft, Gates broke up on a stage.

Earlier, he had grinned his way through a speech to his employees in Redmond, telling them he was confident the company would prevail on appeal. But he was overcome with emotion later in the day as he gave a speech to a group of Gates Millennium Scholars, a select group of minority students who will attend college as recipients of a grant from the Gates Foundation.

As he addressed the scholars, Gates looked around at the audience, which included many close friends and members of his family, and he could not speak. "I was just thinking about my dad supporting me, and my mom not being there," Gates recalled later. And as he took in the enormity of everything that was in front of him, and what had happened to him, his voice cracked, his eyes teared up, and the richest man in the world had to summon all his strength he could just to keep talking.

Gates always figured he would focus on giving away his fortune when he hit his 50s or 60s. Before she died of cancer in 1994, Mary Gates always preached the importance of "giving back," and Gates always figured he would get around to it when he had more time. But at 45, Gates has sped his timetable significantly. Why? It was a confluence of factors, he said: His wife's and father's impetus, his personal fortune soaring to levels he could have never foreseen, and the urgency to combating so many of the global health menaces. Part of Gates's increased sensitivity was stirred by having his own children. "The idea of the health of a child is so much more poignant when you talk about it in terms of somebody that people know," he said.

On another level, Gates's willingness to do something as ambitious as trying to save millions of lives comports to one of the common motivations inherent to this book's protagonists: a desire for, perhaps an addiction to, the notion of finding out exactly what he is capable of. It helps to have a phenomenal growth sector to attack, such as software, or a ridiculous net worth—say $70 billion—to attack with. But it is also central to a personality that seems incapable of niche markets, small gestures, or limited ambitions.

For as much as one can question the motives of anyone who gives away $23.5 billion, some have ascribed Gates's stepped-up giving to an attempt at image repair. "The most expensive PR initiative in history," said one Silicon Valley rival. But whether intended or not, Gates's recent gifts have served as tidy antidotes to the battered Bill Gates brand—a balm to the demonization from his rivals and government, as well as the standard resentments that come with having more money than anyone else.

Some icons seem born into a natural spotlight; the role suits the broad shoulders of a Ted Williams neatly. Not Gates. He is not so much larger-than-life or smaller-than-life as he is, simply, programmed for higher speeds and functionality. Thus, in the whole of the wired package, Gates is smarter-than-life, faster-than-life, weirder-than-life. I've never been in a room with a person who exudes more nervous energy than Gates. It's as if his mind were charged to a degree that moves his body. It's a fascinating thing to watch him churn, intimidating, too, knowing that anything you say could instantly be dubbed the stupidest fucking thing that Bill Gates had ever heard.

But to watch him on stage, in a hero's setting, tends to reinforce the impression of Gates's basic discordance with the world he's changed. I remember watching Gates as he slumped his way through a series of public love-ins in New York in December 2000. The events were all tied to a $100-million gift Gates had given to the Boys and Girls Clubs of America. The formal presentation of the gift took place at the Boys and Girls Club of Central Harlem, in a gymnasium packed with children, media, and dignitaries.

Before Gates arrived, a clot of elected officials waded through the crowd and onto the stage—Senator Charles Schumer (D-NY), Senator Joseph Biden (D-Del.), Representative Charles Rangel (D-NY). None of them got the rock star gasps that Gates did as he walked in last, accompanied by Hillary Rodham Clinton.

The politicians gave speeches praising the benefactor. Biden led the room in a standing ovation; Schumer compared Gates to Andrew Carnegie; Boys and Girls Club member Naisha Boles declared Gates's then-recent book *Business @ The Speed of Thought* to be "a phenomenal piece of literature."

As Gates sat surrounded on stage, he looked an odd hybrid of awkward and serene, smiling while seemingly braced for a light fixture to fall on his head. He wore a gray suit, and he sat with his legs crossed and his hands folded daintily on his lap. He was, notably, not rocking—something he appeared to be working not to do.

In an interview I did with Gates a few weeks later, he spoke about how much he loved having Ballmer along with him atop his company. "It's a lot less lonely with the two of us than if there were just one of us," he said. "I don't know how guys do it just alone." But it's still lonely, he reiterated, in ways that are hard to convey. And as I watched him on stage, the empty space to his sides seemed apparent. He looked, at this moment, lonely.

"It's a great time to be a kid," Gates said in his speech in Harlem. He read haltingly from a script—"We've pursued our optimism!"—and received a standing ovation when he was done and the ceremony ended.

As the politicians shook hands with everybody, Gates walked briskly through the gym with a frozen smile on his face. He bee-lined to the exit and managed to get out the door without touching a single person in the crowd, even by accident.

CHAPTER FIVE

STEVE CASE

The Upgrade

As he absorbed the pinnacle event of his career, America Online founder and CEO Steve Case seemed not himself.

It was a Sunday night, January 9, 2000. AOL, the perennially left-for-dead online service, was close to buying Time Warner, the biggest media company in the world. Case and ten members of the company's board of directors convened in a room in the thirtieth floor of a Manhattan law firm; a twelfth director was connected by speakerphone. Eighteen investment bankers, lawyers, and AOL staffers sat on the perimeter.

Negotiators for AOL and Time Warner had agreed to terms on the deal three nights earlier, and final issues were now being volleyed: pricing, management teams, tax, and accounting arcana. "How's this gonna work, fellas?" director Gen. Colin Powell asked on the subject of a proposed dual-headquarters arrangement in New York and Virginia. A buffet sat untouched. Vice chairperson Ken Novack dozed, wasted from marathon negotiations over the weekend. One lawyer's leg quivered, to the annoyance of those around him.

Every era has an event or image to embed its zeitgeist in history—a market crash, Woodstock, or Nixon's salute. But to this point, the so-called Internet age did not have one. It had plenty of strangeness, virtual wealth, new toys; a procession of Netscape-like IPOs, books with titles like *Dow 36,000* and "the Web-will-make-you-obsolete-or-rich" claims. But no singular "pinch-me" moment. And really, this lack of a tangible focal point seemed fitting to the moment. The hovering notion: Who knew what would be left after this bender, anyway?

But this was real, as real as the portrait of *Time* founder Henry Luce that would soon hang in Steve Case's office. While so many Internet standouts—Yahoo, Excite, Amazon—were suspended blissfully in lucrative states of pure possibility, Case was ready to cash in. He would trade AOL's speculative allure for the lasting security of real-world media domination. He would be insulated by Time Warner's massive portfolio of assets—its CNN, its Warner Brothers Studios, its cable lines, all of its grown-up legitimacy, and, hooo boy, all the mainstream respect that Case had always craved.

This was so real that it was *surreal*.

Case sat mid-table in the CEO's seat, his face flush and relaxed. "Steve had such a look of serenity," said board member Frank Caulfield a few weeks later. "You'd have no idea we were about to consummate the biggest deal in history."

Indeed, his manner defied the mania in the room and the usual Case. Like many successful executives, he never trusted success and could certainly never enjoy it. His mind seemed to be constantly churning with scenarios of unknown entrepreneurs, unformed companies, and uninvented technologies blowing up his whole creation tomorrow. Now, though, Case's jaw was not clenched nervously; his baby-round eyes were not opened wide or narrowed in suspicion; and his general bearing did not evoke a scared comic-book character. Case seemed to be in the midst of some real-time transformation—just as the media world would be undergoing, thanks to him.

AOL's board voted unanimously for the merger. Time-Warner's board voted shortly afterward. The two groups were connected by speakerphone, and applause cracked over the lines when their agreement was dubbed official. Case, whose personal coming of age has mirrored that of his embattled company, was suddenly in charge of all this awesome chaos. He indulged a flash of satisfaction. His face was a flush red, his words breezy. He lapsed into dopey smiles.

"At that moment," recalled board member James Barksdale, former head of Netscape, "Steve seemed to be completely above it all."

Case could relax, but not forget. Over the last decade, according to industry sources, Case felt that executives at Time Warner had given him little respect in a series of dealings. He would walk away from meetings in a slow burn, uttering variations on, "Those guys will work for us one day."

Shortly after the Time Warner deal was set, at least two Case associates—one a former AOL executive, the other a high-level official at another technology company—told me they had conversations with Case in which he recalled past slights from Time Warner. He wore a Cheshire cat grin when the deal was at hand, a look that one Time Warner official compared with a kid who just beat his dad at chess for the first time.

Case is too pragmatic to bog down in revenge. Or at least admit to it. When I asked him about his recollection of Time-Warner's past dismissals of AOL, he said, "No, no, no," and added that Time Warner officials had treated him with more respect over the years than executives at other media companies did.

In any event, when AOL and Time Warner announced their $112-billion merger on January 10, 2000, Case and Levin declared their union a "merger of equals." It was not. AOL shareholders would own 55 percent of the merged company, and it was clear how the deal would be reported and remembered.

AOL buys Time Warner.

"This had to be particularly sweet for Steve," said one former AOL executive who left the company in 1998. "He tries to come off like he doesn't care about these competitive things. But the man is always keeping score. This was his ultimate victory."

STATURE

In his corporate persona, Steve Case always sought to evoke the aw-shucks self-assurance of a summering frat boy. He had a gawky adolescent posture, a lazy, matter-of-fact cadence to his speech. As with so much at AOL, the Case image was carefully crafted to evoke a fun, freewheeling feel. Case was "cool," in the practiced manner of "the "cool" they teach the MBAs zigzagging the AOL lobby in expensive casual clothing.

But up close, there is very little that's inviting about Case. In conversation, his body language turns fidgety. His stony face can be unnervingly hard to read. Around AOL, he is known as "the Wall."

Mark Walsh, a former AOL executive, recalls a trip he took with Case a few years ago to a county fair in Ossining, New York. They'd each had a beer or three, and Case became woozy after a loop-the-loop ride. His expression never changed as he excused himself, walked into the woods, and returned two minutes later. "I just vomited," Case said in a dim monotone, and then proceeded to the next ride. "Now that's focus," Walsh marveled.

Walsh remembered the first time he met Case. Walsh ran an online shopping service, CUC International, and the two men had just struck a deal after a protracted haggle. When Walsh got up for the post-deal handshake, he noticed a photo of a college campus in Case's office. "Is that the University of Virginia?" Walsh asked.

"No," Case answered briskly. He did not volunteer that it was his alma mater, Williams College. "Steve never tells you anything that you don't need to know."

Almost as soon as the deal with Time Warner was struck, friends and associates noticed a change in Case. He was on myriad magazine covers. He was being dubbed "Citizen Case," and receiving congratulatory calls from world leaders and spontaneous applause from rooms full of AOL employees. But Case's above-it-all manner in the board meeting presaged a new executive bearing. He wanted to become more of an emissary, come off more stately and dignified, lose the edgy bearing of the underdog.

When Case and his Time Warner counterpart, Gerald Levin, were negotiating the merger's provisions, Case said he had no interest in being CEO of the combined company. This was unusual, since the CEO's job usually offered the most power and control. But Case didn't want power and control so much as he craved stature. He wanted the loftier, more patriarchal role of chairman. Let Levin endure the day-to-day rigors while Case surfed above his empire, transmitting huge thoughts, focusing on long-term strategy, getting his name on buildings. He would preach the good and power of "media integration." He would meet with world leaders and politicians, trading his khakis and Hawaiian shirts for solemn gray suits.

The PR initiative seemed to be: "Make Steve chairmanlike."

A few weeks after AOL's merger with Time Warner was announced, Case visited the offices of *The Washington Post* for a lunch meeting with a group of reporters, editors, and *Post* executives. He had done this every few years and had always been particularly guarded, even by the hypercautious standards, and those of CEOs who venture into a room full of journalists and sit at a table full of tape recorders. He had longstanding animosity for the *Post*, AOL's hometown newspaper, which he felt had run unfairly critical coverage of his company over the years. When AOL was young and struggling, Case worked hard to forge content partnerships with The Washington Post Company—the local epitome of mainstream, old-media credibility—only to be rebuffed. The luncheon had the feel of a triumphant return. But this was a visibly loosened-up version of Case.

He wore a pressed blue dress shirt and bright yellow tie. His haircut appeared more expensive than it used to. He had the look of someone who was on TV a lot.

Case repeated the requisite post-deal "merger of equals" cliches ("This isn't about AOL buying Time Warner, or Time Warner buying AOL. This is about changing the world"). He spoke about "building a medium we can all be proud of," about how he wanted the merged entity to be "the most valuable, most respected company in the world." The kinds of things he'd been saying daily for four weeks.

But every so often, Case betrayed his signature sarcasm, a caustic edge that was never hard to elicit from him. Alan Spoon, who was then the CEO of The Washington Post Company, prefaced a question with, "Recently, the *Washington Post* reported," to which Case interrupted, "Oh, does that make it true?" He spoke with a baiting tone, sounding a little too hostile for it to be just a chummy nudge.

AN UNDISPUTED GENERAL

It was around this period, March 2000, that I began doing research on Case's life for a profile I was writing about him for the *Post*. While Case might now be the chairman of the largest media conglomerate in the world, he never had much use for the press—and less use for stories like this: The Life Story. There were so many unpredictable areas, unsettled topics, uncontrolled scenarios. Before the *Post* luncheon, I earnestly explained to Case what I was doing, even though he'd been fully briefed. When I said I planned to interview about one hundred people who have known him, he winced, as anyone would. He needed this like he needed a hernia.

Case agreed to a one-hour sit-down discussion, in which he strenuously stuck to the AOL official story—stuff he'd said before, and that had been reported, many times over. He agreed to

speak to me only on the condition that I not quote him on anything without his approval before publication. This "interview"
took place at a conference table in his office beginning at 3 P.M.
Case ate a banana and handfuls of jelly beans from a jar. He was
clearly impatient with any attempt to get him to talk about himself. Why was his history the least bit relevant to anything? His
life's imperative was now the future.

At precisely 4 P.M., the AOL public relations woman, who
babysat the interview, coughed slightly—that "time's up" cough
they teach in PR school—and within a few seconds, Case was
again safe behind his terminal, barely managing goodbye.

This was where Case spent much of his time, ensconced in
his Spartan fifth-floor suite at AOL's Dulles, Virginia campus. The
office was large, with a picture-window view of planes taking off
and landing at Dulles Airport. Case passed hours there alone. He
bunkered behind his terminal, pondering, and dispatching long
e-mails to his staff.

At the suggestion of AOL's PR people, I followed up my
interview with Case by e-mail. It would be such a cool and appro-
priate way to communicate with the senior titan of new media,
they said. But of course, e-mail is also a perfect way to control an
encounter. It eliminated all the vagaries of human interaction.
What Case wasn't sure about, he could vet with his PR chief, who
would be copied on all incoming and outgoing e-mails.

Case was protected. And, just in case, everything he wrote in
his e-mails would be considered off the record. If I wanted to
quote from any of them, he would have to approve it first.

In one e-mail, Case described himself this way: "I am equal
parts capitalist (building a big successful business), an anarchist
(enjoying blowing things up and starting over), and populist (really
hoping to make the benefits of this medium available to everyone)." This was about as expansive as Case got with me, and it
seemed a decent summation of his business self. Indeed, Case was

the ultimate mainstream revolutionary, an unconventional thinker from a conventional suburban world who was bent on mass-market domination. This mimicked his essential map for success at AOL: He sold his service as a safe-for-Middle-America way to experience an online world that seemed slightly exotic, anarchic.

Case was a diligent e-mailer. I would usually ask a few questions per e-mail and, within a few hours, even on Sundays, he would e-mail me back. It was an efficient way to communicate, if not usually revealing. There were paragraphs that could have been written by PR ("The best is yet to come—most of AOL's history lies in its future!"). He used a lot of exclamation points and signed everything "SC."

After a multiple e-mail afternoon, Case ended one missive by saying, "Now would you just shut up and finish the damn piece?" That was as close as I got to a friendly aside from Case.

Several of my AOL-arranged interviewees stressed Case's philanthropic ventures and his meetings with world leaders. At one point, I asked AOL's then-PR chief, Kathy Bushkin, a former Gary Hart press secretary, if she could help find some old Case friends for me to interview. How tricky could such a request be? Who wouldn't want to round up a few old pals to testify on his behalf? But AOL offered up only dignitaries: Colin Powell, an array of current and former CEOs—Tribune Corp's Scott Smith— big boys, all of them. They seemed to admire Case enough, but none appeared to know him that well. Powell speculated that he thought Case would make a good general.

This much was evident: Steve Case was now an undisputed general of the Internet age, era, century, whatever, and he was determined to act that way. He owned a superpower portfolio of brands. No one in high-tech could rival his juggernaut in terms of power, influence, and reach. Except for Bill Gates.

There's always Bill Gates. Case watched him closely. They had a lot in common. Both grew up in wealthy families, the sons of strong mothers and prominent lawyer fathers in the Western United States—Case in Honolulu, Gates in Seattle. Both their childhoods were marked by fierce competitions, often at family retreats; both later dabbled in politics (Case as a college political science major, Gates as a congressional page); they went on to marry executives at their companies. They are co-founders and longtime CEOs who, within three days of each other in January 2000, announced they would give up day-to-day responsibilities of their companies and become chairmen.

But for as similar as their backgrounds are, there is one big figurative difference in the worlds they came from. "Bill was a boy prodigy from the beginning," says Greg Maffei, a former Microsoft executive who knows both men. "Steve obviously spent a lot of time in the wilderness trying to fight his way out."

Like AOL and unlike Microsoft, Case has struggled to win acceptance in a world quick to overlook him. He always measured himself against larger, powerful personalities and institutions. Early in his life, there was his older brother, Dan Case III, who would go on to be one of the world's foremost technology investment bankers. Later, Case took on a formidable array of naysayers, mentors, and competitors. This struggle has bred in him an aggressive sense of how to find daylight, burrow free of crowded markets, and forge precedents as he goes.

It explained, to some degree, how someone like Case was driven to build an empire—and how a boy outcast could become an icon of faceless communication.

CASE RULES

Early in their marriage, Dan Case and his wife, Carol, were told they could not have children. The couple, in their twenties, had planned a big family, continuing the legacy of large Case clans among Hawaii's Anglo establishment. Both were fourth-generation islanders—Dan the great-great-grandson of a lawyer who had come from Topeka, Kansas, in the late 1890s, Carol the descendant of a sugar plantation owner who had emigrated from England.

Dan and Carol Case filed papers that led to their adopting a newborn girl, Carin, a few months after they had learned that Carol was pregnant. Dan Case III was born five months later, the miracle baby.

Steve Case followed thirteen months later, on August 21, 1958, the day Hawaii was granted statehood.

Dan worked long hours as a corporate lawyer while his wife, who quit teaching to raise her three diapered children, ran a taut household: strict mealtimes, mandatory quiet periods, and, as they grew older, regular chores. Jeff, the fourth child, arrived four years after Steve.

When Steve was 8, the family moved to a cul-de-sac in the Manoa Valley section of Honolulu. Their street, Ahualani Place, comprised nine households—seven Caucasian, one Japanese, one Korean—and everyone knew everyone else.

It was an idyllic setting to grow up in, a place steeped in the picket-fence suburban ethos that Steve would stay so attuned to in his business career. The Case children began sunny days to the song of tropical birds. If the wind was blowing up the hill, they might hear the recital of the Pledge of Allegiance on the lawn of the nearby Punahou School, an exclusive private school where Carol had taught and which all four Case kids would attend from kindergarten through twelfth grade. There were corgis named Tuffy and Tabe in the house, and coin collections, swims in the neighbors' pools, summers at a beach rental, and Sundays at the Congregationalist Central Union Church, where the boys were ushers. They partook of a classic TV diet of the age, often rushing to get their homework done so they could catch "Batman," "Gilligan's Island," "Get Smart," or "Hawaii 5-0."

These were the dark ages before chat rooms and instant messaging, when kids called one another together by bouncing a basketball on a driveway. After school, the sound would echo across the cul-de-sac. Steve heard the bouncing from his bedroom, where he was often tinkering with a toy rocket or hatching a mail-order business or listening to the Rolling Stones. He spent so much time upstairs that his family called Steve's room his "office." He spent hours alone there, typing letters or ordering stuff from scientific catalogues. He loved nothing more than getting mail.

But Steve would heed the call of the basketball as the neighbor kids gathered, along with Dan and Jeff, at the hoop mounted on the Alexander family's garage. A contest seemed to bring out Steve's feistier alter ego, an out-of-nowhere tenacity.

Losing came tough to the Case boys, particularly Steve and Dan, who waged a quietly vehement rivalry. "The games would almost get bloody," says Steven Bond, who lived around the corner. "There was always more of the physical, territory-grabbing stuff with Steve and Danny."

It didn't matter whether the Case boys were competing as teammates or against each other. If they were losing, they would sometimes change the rules, prompting a joke among the other children. "We used to call it Case Rules," recalls another neighbor, Lucy Alexander Black.

The games would rage just before dinner, serving as prolonged study breaks. "Steve displayed a style of savvy and steadiness that always made him a very deceptive player," Doug Alexander recalled in an e-mail. He would sometimes celebrate an important basket by breaking into Steve Martin's "happy feet" routine, shuffling his feet uncontrollably. "We'd follow Steve's lead with wiggling and shaking that must have resembled a muted version of 'Dance Fever,'" Alexander said.

When Steve and Dan were teammates, "they always seemed to know exactly where the other one was going to pass or jump,"

Steven Bond said. When they were opponents, Dan would get particularly fierce, Bond said. "There was no way he was going to lose out to his younger brother."

"We figured since we were out there playing, we might as well win," said Steve Case.

Dan was clearly the most competitive Case, the one most likely to invoke Case Rules, said Lucy Alexander Black. But she and other neighbors recall that Case Rules were a family trait, cited in numerous games. "They would sometimes move the out-of-bounds lines in croquet," she says. "Anything to give the Case boys an edge."

Basketball would end when Mrs. Case rang the dinner bell and her sons retreated to their home with big glass doors and a view of the Honolulu skyline and the Pacific Ocean. Inside, games would also abound—cribbage, checkers, chess. Steve had a penchant for the board game, Risk, where the object was world domination.

The Case games were often spiced by gentle wagers ("Loser does the dinner dishes"), but the parents forbade cash bets. "They never minded doing the dishes so much as they just hated losing," Carol Case said. She and Dan, Sr. encouraged the competition, as long as it included fair play. Dan, Sr. bought boxing gloves for the kids to work out disputes in a safe forum with prescribed rules. He always preached, "Humble in victory, gracious in defeat."

When there was nothing to compete in, Steve was adept at creating diversions. He liked gadgetry: cameras and weather stations, then radio and cassette recorder gizmos. With Dan, he developed an early fixation on selling. They launched businesses together, selling Dixie cups full of limeade when they were 7 and 6, and expanding into door-to-door sales of greeting cards and garden seeds.

Steve and Dan once secured exclusive Honolulu rights to sell a particular brand of Swiss watch—and sold zero watches. Dan said they never embarked on childhood business ventures for the money, but for the gamesmanship of it. "Money's just the way we kept score," he said. Steve would stay up late, dreaming up schemes, sometimes waking Dan with ideas.

Dan was a classic firstborn: an A student, class president, and do-gooder. Once, a basketball game was interrupted by the sound of a car crashing on the main road, a few hundred yards from the cul-de-sac. Dan, then 16, charged to the scene and was directing traffic within seconds. "Danny was a perfect role model, very upstanding," Steven Bond says. "Steve was always cooking things up and looking for a niche."

Steve met his brother's precedent by detouring around it. "I defined the market early in our family through achievement," Dan says. "Steve was the third guy up. He had to work to define his own path." Steve was a B-plus student and indulged a love of rock-and-roll as a music critic for the high school paper ("Aerosmith . . . completely overwhelmed the audience and made the Guess Who look, by comparison, like a high-school dance band"). He wrote to record labels and convinced them that the paper was one of Hawaii's biggest-circulation papers for young people—this was technically true—and he received free albums.

Dan and Steve say their rivalry was manageable, but there were collisions, such as a fight when they were 13 and 12. Dan can't remember what started it, only that afterward he vowed never to fight his brother again. They were getting too big. "There is a bad risk–reward here," he recalled saying to Steve. "One of us is going to get hurt, and it's going to hurt our friendship."

So the Case brothers worked to "manage potential areas of conflict," Dan said. Both loved tennis, and it became conceivable, given their closeness in age and the insular world they inhabited, that they would have to play each other in tournaments. They negotiated a deal: Steve agreed to relinquish tennis; Dan gave up basketball.

In the mid-1970s, Dan was contemplating a number of eastern colleges, including Williams College, the liberal arts school in

198 STEVE CASE The Upgrade

the northwest corner of Massachusetts, that his father had attended. It came as a surprise when Steve staked a claim to family convention and asked Dan to leave Williams for him. Dan obliged and chose Princeton University, where he solidified his stellar credentials while Steve went on to become a campus maverick in the Berkshires.

A MEANS TO AN END

He was not a political agitator or prankster. "He was that guy from Hawaii who was always trying to sell stuff," says Larry Sisson, a Williams classmate who now works at Microsoft. "A classic huckster," says Williams professor Mark Taylor.

Case set up tables in the mail room to sell fruit baskets and ran a shuttle service to the airport. He went about his businesses with the manic edge of a man unleashed. As soon as he could think of a market niche, he tried to conquer it.

He was no longer confined to the small-scale aims of his boyhood, business peddled door-to-door or by mail order. As a practical matter, there wasn't much else to do. Williams was an especially sleepy place in the years Case attended, 1976 to 1980. There were few memorable events. Bo Derek came to Williams to film a scene from *A Change of Seasons,* and students were paid $35 to be extras (Derek averaged a "7" in a poll of campus men). One night, members of the rugby club got drunk and threw an inflatable doll off the Sawyer Library balcony, inciting a large student protest against sexism.

Case was aggressive in business, but not in personality. He was generally well liked and carried out his sales offensives with little rancor. But this changed when he applied his ambitions to the campus entertainment committee, which he joined in his sophomore year, 1977. Music was the one medium that truly excited

STEVE CASE The Upgrade **199**

Case as a young man. He began trying to bring headline acts to this rock-and-roll backwater three hours northwest of Boston. "Steve said, 'We're changing the paradigm, we're going to get Springsteen and the Cars to play the Williams hockey rink,'" says John Svoboda, Case's collaborator on the committee and now a venture capitalist in Chicago. "The student government body was always pleading with me to rein this guy Case in."

There was concern that if these big acts actually came to Williams, it would bankrupt the entertainment committee. Case argued that he could make more money for the college by putting on a successful show.

Upon being vetoed, Case would listen, shrug, and try again. He adopted a strategy of booking cheaper bands he believed were approaching stardom, an early willingness to anticipate Next Big Things. He signed the then-unknown Cheap Trick (for $1,250) and Meat Loaf ($500). It wasn't his fault that both wound up canceling Williams for bigger gigs.

In his senior year, Case organized a Saturday night show at a student club, The Log, that featured two cover bands, The Vans (derived from the Cars) and The The. The Vans included the best three musicians Case could find—with himself as front man, despite a singing ability that the *Williams Record* described as "limited."

"Case's dazed and dissatisfied look complemented the band's punk sound," the review said. After eight songs, the Vans left the stage to drunken applause, changed their clothes, and returned as The The.

On many weekends Case would borrow a car and drive an hour to Smith College in Northampton, Massachusetts, to see a girl from New Jersey, Joanne Barker, whom he had met when she was a visiting student at Williams. In class, as in high school, Case was not a great student, earning B's. "He was not someone who stood out as someone who would leave his mark on the world," said Taylor, who is the director of the Center for Technology in the Arts and Humanities at Williams.

Case took Computers 101 his senior year and was miserable. "This was the punch-card age," Case wrote to me in an e-mail. "Waiting an hour to have the cards run to see if the program worked didn't have much appeal."

Case never cared much about circuitry. He had loved Estes rockets and weather stations as a boy, and then radio and cassette recorder contraptions and cutting-edge photography equipment. But he was always less interested in how things worked than in what they could do. "I always saw technology as a means to an end," he wrote. "I have always tried to understand enough about the technology to be able to understand what might be possible, while maintaining a certain distance."

This distills a Case peculiarity among high-tech founders. He is not, nor did he ever claim to be, an inventor or programming whiz. While his titan counterparts—Bill Gates, Larry Ellison, Steve Jobs—were all fixated on circuitry, Case gazed into machines and saw a potential marketplace first. That became his frontier, his purpose in a box, and it compensated for one of his essential oddities: Case was the rare, introverted marketer. He was a marketing nerd.

Williams did not offer marketing classes, so Case majored in what he considered the closest thing, political science. He cast his first presidential vote in 1980, for independent John Anderson.

The most enduring lessons of Case's college years were self-taught. He spent hours in the library, reading marketing trade publications, especially *Advertising Age*. He also read Alvin Toffler's *The Third Wave*, a treatise that posited a world where machines communicated with one another. Case had already come to view this world as inevitable, not futuristic. His interest in gadgetry was growing into a fascination with interactive electronics.

Cable television was in few homes in the late 1970s, but Case kept hearing about its possibilities of hundreds of channels and two-way communication. In 1979, he spent the summer selling cable TV subscriptions door to door for Oceanic Cable on Oahu. He talked his boss into letting him run a cable wire through the neighbor's yard and into the Case house. That summer, Case's father took him to a Rotary Club speech by a brash cable TV executive named Ted Turner, who had just completed the Trans Pacific Yacht Race. "I was enthralled and captivated," Case recalled. "He seemed like the classic entrepreneur to me, swinging for the fences with seeming fearlessness."

As he prepared to leave Williams, Case applied to a host of MBA programs and was turned down by them all. He also sought marketing jobs at large corporations. But the options in interactive media were small, even if Case's plans were not. In her book *AOL.com* author Kara Swisher quotes from a cover letter Case wrote to Time Inc.'s new cable property, Home Box Office: "Innovations in telecommunications (especially two-way cable systems) will result in our television sets (big screen, of course!) becoming an information line, newspaper, school, computer, referendum machine and catalogue."

But he was rejected and didn't get to meet the executive who ran HBO, a Time fast-tracker named Gerald Levin.

ACTUALLY DOING IT

While Dan Case studied at Oxford University on a Rhodes scholarship, Steve set his sights on a job at Procter & Gamble Co., known as a great training ground for marketers. Procter & Gamble, too, rejected Case, but he returned to Cincinnati at his own expense and finagled another interview.

This persistence—showing up and occupying a space until it became his—would characterize Case's career. While the tendency could be as annoying as it was endearing, it usually worked. Procter & Gamble hired Case as an assistant brand manager.

As a philosophy, Procter & Gamble espoused exhaustive market research and focus groups; the company preached and revered the power of the "brand" to win customer loyalty, be it for Duncan Hines cake mix, Pringle's potato chips, or Crisco. It was a marketing belief system that informed a generation of New Economy executives: Around the time Case was there, Procter & Gamble was also home to future CEOs of General Electric (Jeffrey Immelt), Intuit (Scott Cook), and Microsoft (Steve Ballmer), among others.

Case was assigned to a product called Abound, a small towel soaked in hair conditioner that could be rubbed directly onto the scalp (slogan: "Towelette, You Bet"). Case launched a point-of-sale marketing program that involved an optical sensor that would activate a demonstration video whenever a customer walked near an Abound display. His boss, Charlotte Otto, recalls the idea as "brilliant," but the contraption was deemed too expensive to deploy.

Case lasted almost two years at Procter & Gamble, longer than Abound lasted in test marketing. He was becoming certain that he had no interest in being boxed into a large corporation long-term. But Pizza Hut, a subsidiary of PepsiCo, was offering him more influence than most people his age were granted—albeit on the nation's pizza tastes. He viewed this as a transitional job, a place to gain experience until he found something more exciting. He spent days and nights lost in rental cars around the country, sampling pizza, studying (tasting) the competition. This was called "competitive defensive marketing," said Ken Lerman, Case's Pizza Hut mentor, and it consisted of grading the nation's pizza with a scientific tally of five taste categories—crust, dough, sauce, cheese, and topping.

Case's parents worried. His father, who has been at the same law firm for forty-nine years, believed that job-hopping would alarm future employers and prospective MBA programs. His brother Dan had returned from England and begun his career at

Hambrecht & Quist, where he became a protege of co-founder Bill Hambrecht and a point man for the bank's work with emerging technology companies. He sent Steve the marketing plans of promising high-tech firms, knowing that he was bored at Pizza Hut and seeking a way out. Steve set up a marketing consultancy on the side. He used Dan's San Francisco address and forwarded Dan's phone—with the Bay Area's 415 area code—to his own in Kansas so he would have more Silicon Valley credibility. The brothers spoke for hours by phone and saw each other often during these years. Steve Case spent solitary nights in a small condominium on East Harry Street in Wichita. His interest in new media tools only grew amid the arid "anywhere" of middle management. Lerman remembers having Case to dinner at his house in Wichita and watching him gawk at a cutting-edge contraption, the VCR, which allowed him to zoom through commercials.

Case bought his first personal computer, a bulky Kaypro. With a modem, he discovered an escape from the isolation: the ability to connect with a small universe of computer users through an early online service, the Source. "It was magical because after thinking about it and reading about it and imagining it, I was actually doing it," Case wrote in an e-mail.

The Kaypro experience was the clunky embodiment of what was suddenly possible—and, given how hard the machine was to use, the work that remained to be done. What Case craved in his early twenties was a way to pursue this mission full time. In 1983, he found one through his older brother.

THE WHIPPERSNAPPER

At a trade show in Las Vegas, Dan Case introduced Steve to Bill Von Meister, the grandiose and erratic founder of Control Video Corp. of Vienna. Virginia Control Video was a computer company that connected set-top TV boxes to Atari games through phone lines; Hambrecht & Quist was one of its backers and Dan Case was a board member. Von Meister offered Steve Case a job as a marketing consultant. The notion of working in high-tech appealed to Case, and he believed that his marketing instincts and skills would convey seamlessly to this new, uncharted realm. He also noted that Pepsi CEO John Sculley had just left the company to work at a hot technology start-up, Apple Computer.

Soon after Case took the job at CVC, the company's investors deposed Von Meister and fired most of the staff, about fifty people. As one of Control Video's few marketing specialists, Case escaped the purge, "definitely on the merits," says Bob Cross, a corporate turnaround specialist who was brought in during the mid-1980s. But there was another factor, too: "We wanted to keep Hambrecht & Quist interested in us," he says, the implication being that they didn't want to alienate Dan Case.

Dan and Steve were known at Control Video as Upper Case and Lower Case. While the distinctions were awarded playfully, and by age, the broader meaning was clear. In 1984, Dan Case stepped away from any involvement with Control Video because of concerns over possible conflict of interest. "People needled Steve about his own brother not believing in him," recalls George Middlemas, a Chicago venture capitalist and early board member. "That had to light a fire under Steve," he says. Case told me, with some annoyance, that any sibling rivalry with Dan had ended years earlier.

Either way, Steve Case, at 25, was essentially leading the marketing efforts of a company struggling to survive.

In 1983 and 1984, the video game market was dying. Control Video's chain of command was in flux, and Case insinuated himself boldly. He helped implement a new strategy geared to personal computer makers. He spent marathon stretches online, trying to gain some understanding of the emerging world there— at that point, a sparse community of fringe hobbyists. Early investor Len Batterson recalls flying in for a meeting in Vienna. "Case was nowhere to be found. I remember asking where he was, and someone said, 'Oh, Steve's upstairs at the keyboard trying to figure this whole thing out.'"

Case was shy, socially clumsy, and intimacy never came easily to him. He was too busy, or simply averse, and his body of girlfriends and close confidants over the years was small. Larry Sisson said he considered Case a "decent friend at Williams, but never too close," and was surprised in 1985 when Case called and asked him to be one of five groomsmen at his marriage to Joanne Barker. It was a medium–big ceremony at a church in Rumson, New Jersey. Dan Case stood as his brother's best man, and Steve gave matching red ties as gifts to each groomsman.

People who knew Case at the time sensed a personality change, at least at work, where he was spending nearly all of his time. He seemed to exude the busyness of a man free at last to try out big notions. And in his rush, Case collided with the sensibilities of older investors, some of whom dubbed him "the Whippersnapper."

"Steve was a very aggressive guy who believed he should have been the top dog after three days," said Marc Seriff, a Control Video founder. "If you prove yourself to Steve, he will treat you as an intellectual equal. It's one thing if he's 25 and you're 25. It's another thing if he's 25 and you're 55. This was not a time when 25-year-olds interacted with 55-year-olds as peers." Especially if the elders already had lost a lot of money on the company, and several of them wanted Case gone.

Jim Kimsey, a Washington entrepreneur who had been brought in as chief executive, argued that Case was the only one in the company who had a bent for marketing, as well as some knowledge of this mysterious marketplace. Kimsey's endorsement saved Case's job, and set in motion a professional co-dependency that would become the formative relationship in Case's career.

CHEESY

In the mid-1980s, the notion that connected computers would become an essential medium seemed, at best, optimistic. But Case held the idea with a fiery certitude.

Usually the engineers, the ones with an intellectual stake in the product, are the truest believers. Case, however, "sold himself as a user," not as a technologist, Seriff said. He came to see the flaws and magic of the online experience at the same time. Bringing this experience to the masses was a quest Case took personally.

After years in the wilderness, thrashing about with elaborate ideas, Case had found his outlet. In 1985, Control Video rechristened itself Quantum Computer Services Inc. It was designed exclusively for the Commodore International Ltd. personal computer, for which Quantum had developed a nighttime service, Q-link, that provided an array of communications tools, games, news, and soap opera updates.

Case applied his occupy-and-conquer approach to sales, driving every week to Commodore's headquarters near Philadelphia to foster the relationship. The next year he moved to Cupertino, California, in an effort to win the business of Apple Computer's Apple II machines. Once inside, Case showed up every day for three months. Finally, Apple officials agreed to let Quantum develop their proprietary online service.

Quantum survived, but the company was always at the mercy of its partners. Its survival depended on how many makers of personal computers Case and Kimsey could persuade to use its fledgling online service. Several people counseled Case to leave the company during this time. The online market was showing little momentum, and a smattering of rivals—particularly Prodigy, with $1 billion from Sears, Roebuck and Co. and International Business Machines Corp.—seemed far more promising.

But Case did not take a single interview with another company. "I felt this was the horse I had bet on, and I felt determined to stick it out," he wrote in an e-mail. By the late 1980s, Case and Kimsey were the public faces of Quantum, a familiar duo in Washington-area business circles. Kimsey, a charismatic backslapper, would calm investors and handle tense negotiations; Case, no backslapper, could project an air of bemused sarcasm that people who didn't know him could find unsettling. But for the most part, Case stayed in the background and focused on strategic planning and marketing.

The commercial Internet was still a few years away, but online users were no longer niche players; the technophiles were being joined by a stream of "early adopters." In 1989, Quantum's service was renamed America Online.

Case was more certain than ever that the online border was finally opening for business and that the companies capitalizing first would prevail. It was, he often would say, a land grab—and he launched a mass mailing of AOL disks to the nation's households. The esoteric community of early online users widely derided his campaign as old-fashioned commercialism. "Cheesy" is a word that was used a lot. But selling to mass markets was something Case had been studying, and perfecting, since boyhood.

"WHAT'S THAT SAYING, ABOUT THE SON NEEDING TO KILL THE FATHER?"

In early 1991, Kimsey entered into merger discussions with CompuServe, a rival online service, and Case made it clear that he would not stay if the deal was completed. It was not (the companies could not agree on a price). But there were other close calls—notably, a near-sale to Microsoft—and Case always argued for independence. He told friends that he worried about "selling out" before he could leave his mark on history.

Case, then 33, was also growing weary of being subordinate to Kimsey. He began agitating for the chief executive's job in late-night phone calls with board members. "Steve always wanted more, and Jim's role was to moderate," says Doug Peabody, a longtime board member. During his phone conversations with Case, Peabody would say, "Look, you're young, you have plenty of time, don't get too out front of yourself." Kimsey himself kept telling Case that he wasn't ready.

At that time, according to several accounts, Case would go around Kimsey and tell people at industry gatherings that he was, in effect, running the company. And he basically was, says John Svoboda, Case's old friend from Williams College, who worked at William Blair, a Chicago investment house that had dealings with AOL in the early 1990s. Svoboda recalls a meeting with Case and Kimsey in which Case was "clearly frustrated" by the setup. "Here was Steve the risk-taker being reined in again by someone who wanted him to move slower."

In 1991, the board finally gave Case the title of chief executive and Kimsey remained as chairman. The company had 130,000 customers by midyear, a fraction of what CompuServe and Prodigy had. Nonetheless, AOL, with just 120 employees, planned an initial public offering early in 1992.

This was not a time when negligibly profitable companies were going public; certainly not firms that had uncertain records and were operating in quirky markets. Still, Case argued for the offering: The company needed cash to expand at the pace he felt necessary. The public offering was also a chance to generate publicity, and Case was anticipating top billing.

But just before the IPO, AOL's directors reasoned that Wall Street would prefer Kimsey's gray eminence to Case's boyish face at the front of the company. They stripped Case of the CEO title. He seethed, but quietly, and several employees protested on his behalf, to no avail.

While Case fit no one's idea of a charismatic leader, he managed to engender a loyal following at AOL, especially among young employees and managers. He worked long hours and endured serial indignities in the name of "building the brand." He would attend countless trade shows, stake out officials from established media companies—like Time Warner and Disney—and beg them to put their content on his online service. They would ignore him, but he would keep coming back.

Many AOL employees viewed Case as an online true believer—the leader of their crusade, especially compared with "businessmen" like Kimsey and some members of the board. His faith gave him credibility with the staff. But Case continued to yearn for recognition as a businessman. "In his own quiet, dogged way, Steve was always crying out for attention from the big boys," said Gary Arlen, an independent Internet analyst in Washington who has known Case for years.

AOL's stock issue, held March 19, 1992, raised $66 million. Case, who had been paid largely in stock options since he left the pizza business, suddenly was worth nearly $2 million on paper. Shortly thereafter, the board returned to him the title of chief executive. He was 34.

But Kimsey remained as AOL's chairman and he continued to cast a paternal shadow over Case. He seemed to relish the role of "mentor" to Case's "protege." He knew Case's sore spots—that Case was insecure about his readiness, about whether he had the stature to lead on his own. Kimsey had his own sensitivities, about being perceived as an "empty suit" within the company, someone who had lucked into a great situation and had no interest in understanding the online world as it grew more complex.

Kimsey often nudged where Case was sensitive. When AOL began drawing attention in the national press, Kimsey would speak about "nurturing" Case. He also would point out that "we hired him because of his brother."

Privately, Kimsey complained that Case never gave him credit for keeping the company alive in the early days. The complaint is echoed by former board members who remain loyal to Kimsey. "Steve has spent a lot of time trying to attribute AOL's ascendancy to his efforts," says George Middlemas, adding that Case's contributions have been "immeasurable" to AOL. "But Steve's not Superman, although he seems to have a need to convey that."

Bottom line, Kimsey said, Case's record speaks for itself. "If I could choose a guy who was gonna make me a billion dollars and a guy who was gonna kiss my—and be grateful, I'd take the first one."

Nursing a scotch in a pink-tinted glass to match his pink shirt and cheeks on a Thursday afternoon in early 2000, Kimsey looked every bit the picture of old-boy Washington. He is reclined in his spacious office suite overlooking the White House and adorned with West Point artifacts. He namedropped several big-name politicians in the course of an hour discussion.

Kimsey is every bit the opposite of Case. He is unrestrained while Case is closed-in; he is old economy to Case's new; self-assured to Case's self-conscious.

If Kimsey was upset over his rift with Case, he hid it. On the rare occasions that he saw Case, Kimsey said the two men were "cordial." He was philosophical.

"What's that saying, about the child needing to kill the father in order to grow up? Maybe there's some of that at work. Maybe it's understandable."

People close to Case defend his loyalty to Kimsey, noting that other executives would have left the company in frustration. In the early 1990s, they mocked Kimsey behind his back for what they felt was his increasing disengagement from AOL. They coined a term, "Where's Kimsey," a play on "Where's Waldo." It was a joke, but Case says that Kimsey's absence had become a serious problem at AOL. Kimsey would have high-level meetings that

Case didn't know about, or say something in the press that would surprise Case.

In an e-mail, Case wrote that in the late 1980s and early 1990s, AOL's executive staff pressed him and Kimsey to clarify their respective jobs. "This was hard for me to deal with," he wrote, "because I was grateful to Jim for the role he played in getting the company started and keeping it alive during our difficult first years. It's unfortunate that a decade later our recollections don't mesh."

The tension between Kimsey and Case crested in November 1995, when Kimsey assumed the largely ceremonial title of chairman emeritus. On the way out, Kimsey told *USA Today* that he planned to bring in an experienced manager to help run the growing company. He was determined, he said, that there be "adult supervision" at AOL in his absence.

COMBAT

Shortly after Kimsey made his "adult supervision" remark, Case was taken out for an Italian dinner in Reston by some other AOL executives. T-shirts printed with the legend "I Need Adult Supervision" were passed around the table, along with "Steve's Troops" caps. Case was given a general's hat.

The show of loyalty came amid one of the most difficult stretches of his life. His eleven-year marriage to Joanne was ending. Then came the news that Case had become involved with AOL Marketing Vice President Jean Villanueva, to whom he now is married. One AOL official remembers Case seeing Villanueva for the first time: She was interviewing for a job at AOL and attending an AOL "beer bust" outside their offices. Case was sitting with Kimsey and asked him who she was. Case then asked if he could be the one to interview her. As years went by, Villanueva became Case's fiercest booster inside AOL.

Case divulged his relationship with Villanueva to the AOL board. The revelation rocked the company. This was a side of Case that few inside AOL, if anyone, knew existed: the emotional, romantic Case. Suddenly, it seemed, the Wall had softened.

Case was hypersensitive to any mention of his marriage ending and his relationship with Villanueva in the press. In April 1996, *Business Week* published a flattering cover story on Case and AOL. But he was furious about the one-sentence mention of him and Villanueva deep in the story, even though news of the relationship had been reported in several places already. According to Swisher's *AOL.Com,* when Case heard that this item would be included, he became apoplectic. He called *Business Week* editors and threatened to take away his previously granted permission for the magazine to use photos from his childhood. "It was like a nuclear explosion," *Business Week* reporter Mark Lewyn, who had known Case and Villanueva for many years, told Swisher. "The vitriol and intensity were remarkable to everyone, since Steve is usually so calm."

People who worked close to Steve Case during that period said he was able to remain focused on his job—and serious issues were mounting at AOL. The rapid acquisition of new users led to a nasty run of technical problems that culminated in late 1996, at which point AOL was becoming known as "America on Hold." Case took the criticism in stride, but it often came with a hint that AOL, by relentlessly marketing a service it could not deliver, was behaving unethically—and this infuriated Case, said one former AOL executive who worked there in that period. "Steve has a strong belief in his own moral correctness," the executive said.

Around this time, AOL decided to tweak its method of accounting, eliminating its long-held and controversial practice of spreading direct marketing costs over a two-year period. Instead, the company would start reporting the costs all at once, causing an immediate hit on the company's earnings—and enraging many on Wall Street. In a prolonged grilling by stock analysts and investors at New York's Essex House hotel, Case fielded every question and never raised his voice. The only time he showed visible strain, according to one eyewitness, was when one questioner dubbed AOL's practices "immoral."

In 1994, 1995, and 1996, AOL recorded its massive disk giveaway as "subscriber acquisition costs," which allowed it to spread the cost over the long term while appearing profitable in the short. (On May 15, 2000, the SEC ruled that AOL should have booked these costs as an "ordinary business expense," and the company agreed to pay a $3.5-million fine to settle the charges; AOL neither admitted nor denied wrongdoing.)

There was more front-office turmoil. In 1996, Case announced that Fed Ex executive Bill Razzouk would join the company as president. He lasted four months, a choice doomed to clashes between Razzouk's conservative operational style and AOL's more wide-open culture. "Bill Razzouk resigned this morning," Case began a meeting with his management team, according to someone in the room. Case looked uncharacteristically shaken in the meeting, his face ashen and his voice pitched.

The Razzouk affair seized on Case's self-consciousness over whether he was in fact mature enough to lead a large and growing organization. "He seemed nervous that all the other adults he had surrounded himself with would lose faith in him," said one executive who has since left the company. Case worried that others would leave, too.

In fact, Case has a strong record of retaining deputies, several of whom have had their pick of chief executive jobs—and this was only partly due to the wealth AOL created for its top ranks. While Case was never big on the basic managerial fuzzies like "thank you's" and "sorry's," his steely determination could prove seductive over time. Examples of this became numerous and well-known within the fledgling sector of online business.

In July 1994, Mark Walsh was preparing to take a job at a Rockville, Maryland-based online service called GEnie. But Case tracked him down to a hotel room in Los Angeles and called him at 6 A.M. L.A. time. "What the [expletive] are you doing?" is how Case greeted his friend, Walsh remembered. By the time Walsh realized who it was, Case had promised that he would wipe out GEnie and that Walsh would be working at AOL within six months. "He was off by three months," recalls Walsh, who stayed at AOL until 1997.

Case was hardly born persuasive. His voice was naturally low, in a way that made it seem like he was straining to reach higher volumes. Case's gift, as always, was his willingness to show up and not go away. And that, essentially, was his message about the online world he was selling: It was here, it wasn't going away, and—he was convinced, call him nuts—it was going to transform the planet.

What people underestimate about Case, board member Frank Caulfield said, was how infectious his intoxication with things online could be over time. "We've all caught the virus, and Steve is the carrier," said Ken Novack.

Case could be hostile toward nonbelievers and dismissive of rivals. As he felt more comfortable in his position, said several longtime associates, his leadership style evolved: from endearing desperation to something that could be viewed as disdainful self-assurance. Scott Kurnit, Chief Executive of About.Com, remembered meeting Case for the first time in 1993 at a convention in Bermuda. Kurnit, then a rising cable executive at Viacom, mentioned to Case that he had taken a job at the online service Prodigy, one of AOL's chief competitors.

"Why the hell are you going to Prodigy?" Case said, Kurnit recalled. "Why the hell didn't you call me?" Case kept shaking his head, and was not smiling. Kurnit tried to lighten the conversation, not successfully. Finally, Kurnit agreed to come to Virginia to meet Case. They met, and had a good discussion, but Kurnit decided that he could not renege on the job at Prodigy.

After the meeting, as Kurnit boarded a shuttle to New York, Case followed him (he was going to New York anyway) and took the seat next to him. He pulled out a contract mid-flight. "Sign this," he said. Kurnit would not and Case didn't react well, Kurnit said, but the two men kept in touch.

In the mid 1990s, Case joined a group of AOL employees at a paintball outing. "He would charge through the woods, crawl on his stomach, run directly into the line of fire," recalls Amy Arnold, a longtime AOL employee who was at the event. At one point, Case took a hit in the face and started bleeding below the eye. He kept playing.

"He was focused on getting the flag," Arnold said, "and he didn't care how he got it."

:-)

Bill Razzouk's job was eventually taken by Bob Pittman, the former head of MTV. Pittman is a social charmer with Hollywood tastes, an image that can obscure a fervidly hands-on management style. He demanded numeric analysis of every aspect of the business (How many people were reading certain pop-up ads for exactly how long?).

Under Pittman's leadership, placards appeared on headquarter's walls to remind everyone of "AOL Valued Work Behaviors" ("team player," "self-management and initiative") and "AOL Valued Leadership Qualities" ("vision," "care for people"). Company mission statements blanketed AOL's offices in various forms (posters, wood carvings). Terms like "core values," "performance-based pressures," and "micro-budgets" became common.

With Pittman in charge, Case could move away from managing the day-to-day operations, a task that never suited him. He tended to lose focus on micro-management matters. He had little skill for, or interest in, basic corporate schmoozing situations. Gary Arlen recalled being invited to a private briefing with Case a few years ago. Arlen brought a business partner and his then 17-year-old son, Benjamin, an AOL user. Arlen recalled that after a perfunctory handshake and a sarcastic remark about Arlen "bringing an entourage," Case didn't acknowledge his son at all.

Case's brilliance lies in his strategic thinking, his ability to discern future market trends and churn endless scenarios through his mind. What were customers ready for? What would his competition do? What if so and so teamed up with so and so? Case's instincts were informed by that rarest of New Economy commodities—experience.

It was also the product of his wiring. "Steve thinks business strategy like there's an eight-dimensional chess game going on in his head," said Marc Andreessen, the co-founder of Loudcloud Inc. and Netscape Communications Inc., who briefly worked at AOL. "Very few people can think that way. It's Steve's form of genius."

In the mid-1990s, the biggest threat to AOL's viability was the Internet. Netscape had released its trademark browser, which allowed personal computer users to "surf" the entire global network. As mainstream users stormed online, the days of proprietary services like AOL seemed numbered. Why would anyone want to play in a little online sandbox when the Internet offered a whole playground?

Case dismissed the notion that the Internet would kill AOL as "Valley talk." It reflected a long-held and mutual ambivalence between Case and the epicenter of the high-tech industry. Silicon Valley's hardcore techies mocked AOL as a pedestrian version of their elite creation, the "Internet on training wheels." Case believed that the Valley's thinking tended toward dazzling technology, often at the user's expense.

Certain high-tech companies and ideas—Apple, eBay, the Linux operating system—foster a ramped-up fanaticism by employees and users. Their inventors—Steve Jobs (Apple), Pierre Omidyar (eBay), Linus Torvolds (Linux)—are often worshipped. But for all the fervor Case held and preached for the "medium," America Online, despite its success, has never incited a religious movement. And that was fine with Steve Case. Customers didn't have to chant "You've Got Mail" as a mantra, just so long as they were comfortable enough to sign up for the service and pay for it.

When Case looked at the Internet, he saw an uncharted wilderness too unruly for the mass markets he'd been studying since Procter & Gamble. What they would want, he believed, was a friendly intermediary.

In 1995, AOL began integrating a Web browser into its service. The transition set off a rush of growth that included the purchases of CompuServe in 1998 and Netscape in 1999. By century's end, nearly 50 percent of home computer users in the United States were getting online through AOL—yet the term "online service" had become all but taboo in Dulles. AOL now viewed itself as a full-blown "media company." Case coined the voracious corporate mantra—AOL Anywhere. He was striving for total ubiquity. Global, preferably. And fast.

Each month, as the company grew, AOL would achieve another milestone, often in relation to some powerhouse that had scoffed at AOL earlier. Case would always take note and keep score.

In 1997, longtime AOL executive Ted Leonsis tried to negotiate a co-branding agreement with Walt Disney Co. "We would never co-brand with a little company like you," a Disney official said, according to a source familiar with the discussions. Leonsis went back and reported the conversation to Case. In late 1998, the source said, shortly after AOL's stock market value exceeded Disney's, Leonsis sent Case an instant message pointing out the benchmark.

Case replied with an emoticon: :-).

STEVE 2.0

Case was now getting picked out in crowds. It always pained him, especially when he was with one of the five children he and Jean had between them. There were threats of harm, AOL sources said, and tightened security measures. Case became accustomed to autograph requests—one of the rituals of the tech-CEO-as-Rock-Star era—which he would usually honor, especially at public events. Once in New Orleans, he was asked to pose for a photo with a married couple who had met on AOL, and he obliged.

His friends and associates remarked that Case seemed noticeably less embattled in the months leading up to the Time-Warner deal. It was as if he could sense that his peak was close. He seemed more reflective, as if he were taking inventory of his career. In September 1999, he gave a brief but sweet testimonial to Kimsey on his sixtieth-birthday video. He came across a Web site for Ken Lerman, his former boss at Pizza Hut, and called Lerman to offer to write something about Lerman on the site. He exchanged sentimental whuda-thunkit e-mails with old AOL friends.

Case brought his wealth and energy to bear on philanthropic projects—and AOL brought its full PR energy to bear on promoting them. Case had proven himself as an entrepreneur, the thinking went. Now he himself deserved to be "branded" on a higher plane.

This is a common transformation among big-ticket technology CEOs. Once they reach a certain level of titanhood, they strive for statesmanhood. Bill Gates did, so did Intel's Andy Grove, Cisco's John Chambers, and others. They were no longer just hugely successful Capitalists, they were now *Industrialists,* posing with world leaders in photos posted on corporate Web sites.

This reinvention was particularly central to Case's character, and in the evolution of how he envisioned himself—or wanted others to see him. He remained loath to be seen as the little brother, friends said. He wanted to be the main man. Or at least a big brother. Case would make unsolicited phones calls of support to the CEOs of young Internet companies as they struggled. "Steve would see some event happen to us, or some article written," said Jeff Bezos, the CEO of Amazon.com. "And he would call and say something like 'Hey, let me tell you a story about our darkest days.'"

Case was also learning to enjoy public life despite himself, a fact many attributed to the influence of Jean Case. "She has helped unlock a part of Steve's personality that you never used to see," said one friend who has known Case for several years. In 1999, when Gerald Levin and Case were among a delegation of U.S. business leaders to visit China, Levin recalls seeing Case and Jean in a "personal moment" outside the palace of Beijing. Steve kept wrapping his arms around her, shrouding her in his jacket to keep her warm. He was surprised by this, Levin said, because it was so at odds with what he perceived as Case's reserve.

A few months later, Case approached Levin on his ultimate land grab: the purchase of Time Warner. After AOL came to dominate access to the Internet, there remained a legion of doubters who insisted that established media interests would figure out how to invade cyberspace and rout AOL. And at a time when anything seemed possible, Case had an acute sense that nothing was secure.

Around that time, John Sidgmore, the vice chairman of Worldcom, remembers watching a panel of CEOs that included Case. "They all kept saying, 'I'm very confident in our strategy,' as if they were certain they knew exactly what they were doing," said Sidgmore, who has known Case for several years. Case said sarcastically that he wished he could be that sure of everything. "To the degree that everything keeps me up, I'm always worried about everything," Case said, according to Sidgmore.

This was especially true in light of AOL's inflated stock value, which Case knew as well as anyone else to be precarious. Joining forces with Time Warner would, in effect, place a floor under AOL's share price, insulating it from the dot-com fallout that was to come. The deal would also bring classic American brands to AOL's empire as the online migration exploded into a cultural revolution. It represented a formal marker for the company's ascendancy—and for Steve Case, it would also represent a bridge between the establishment world he came from and the world he helped create.

Negotiations between Case and Levin ran hot and cold through the end of 1999. The biggest point of contention was the "exchange ratio" between AOL and Time Warner shares—how much each company's market valuations had been skewed, for better (AOL's shares) or worse (Time Warner's) by the peaking dot-com mania. Their negotiations culminated on Thursday, January 6 at a dinner at Case's home in McLean, Virginia. There were impasses, but Novack urged Case and Levin to keep talking. They did, working their way through a bottle of 1990 Bordeaux. As the chocolate mousse dishes were being cleared from the living room, the two men had the broad outlines of a deal.

By the time Jean dropped Case at Dulles Airport on Saturday, the deal was nearly set. He shared a corporate jet with Colin Powell. They discussed leasing a helicopter for future hops to New York, where the AOL and Time Warner conglomerate would be based.

It's a media cliche that if an executive is dressed in casual attire, it signifies the post-adolescent energy of a New Economy company—in other words, a good thing, at least in the late 1990s. If he wears a suit, he works for a company with too much "adult supervision." So it was exhaustively documented that Levin, the then 60-year-old head of old media Time Warner, wore an open collar at the announcement while Case wore the suit and tie. It was a symbol that the new kids had formally usurped the old boys and all that.

But most striking to those involved was Case's show of emotion as he hugged and high-fived his way across the stage. "I tend to intellectualize history as it's happening," Levin said, "but Steve seemed truly touched by the significance of what he had done."

Case would preside over an empire that included the Bugs Bunny cartoons of his boyhood Saturday mornings, the REM CDs he listens to today, one early cable visionary who inspired him as a college student (Ted Turner), and another whose company rejected him for a job (Levin). New media and old, maverick and mainstream, would coexist as a singular corporate powerhouse, a big and uncertain hunk of turf that Case rules.

CHARACTER ISSUES

At the end of my research on Steve Case, I finally encountered a more unvarnished version of the man. He made himself available for a last-minute fact-checking interview on the Friday before the Sunday *The Washington Post* story I was writing on him would be published. This was classic Case: to be inaccessible and reveal nothing until it became apparent what the other person knew. This way, he could see how much information he owned, what kind of control he had. Then he would respond, aggressively.

I reviewed all the objective facts in the story with Case over the phone. In the interest of giving Case advance notice, I read him passages that might have bothered him on Sunday. It was, on the whole, I thought, a profile that gave him his due. But he quibbled on small things, increasingly as the phone call went on.

And bigger things. He raised his voice. He objected avidly to the notion that he had grabbed too much credit for AOL's success.

That he somehow felt vindicated when AOL bought Time Warner.

That he had undermined his bosses.

And any hint that he was ever an upstart seemed a bitter disappointment to him. He repeated his father's bromide "Humble in victory, gracious in defeat" three times.

But by the end of the discussion, Case had returned to an unemotional monotone. He seemed to have come to some peace that this was, at worst, an annoyance.

We hung up. I went to lunch.

When I returned, there was a long voice-mail awaiting me from Case. The more he thought about it, the more upset he was about the "character issues" that people were raising about him in the story. "I've made mistakes, and I will continue to make mistakes, and I am committed to doing things the right way," he said. His tone was at once resigned and pleading. "At the very least, you need to talk to more people," he said to me. I'd spoken to about one hundred already, I told him. He suggested board members Frank Caulfield and Ken Novack, two older mentor types, both of whom I'd spoken to already at length.

Later, Case called again. "Kathy Bushkin said I should call and talk about some philanthropic work we're doing," he said in a flat, obligatory tone, like a kid whose mother was making him call his grandmother to thank her for a lousy present. He left his cell phone number and his hotel room in Atlanta. I called him back and we talked more.

There were no ground rules for these discussions. They were on the record. But it was too close to publication for me to introduce too much new Case material into the newspaper story—except for his responses to specific characterizations, or corrections to objective facts. If I could do the story again, I would have figured out a way to use more. This was as revealing a set of conversations as I could have hoped for with Case. It offered a neat glimpse of his sensitivities, his control-freakishness, his edges when he feels cornered.

When I read him Kimsey's remark about the son needing to kill the father, Case did a decidedly unCase-like thing—he gasped. Slightly, but audibly. "That's bizarre," Case said. Was I sure Kimsey said that? Surely I misquoted him. He suggested that I call Kimsey again to double-check. I did. ("It's a line I've used many times," Kimsey said.)

People had told me that Kimsey always knew how to faze the unfazable Case. Still, I was amazed at the vehemence of Case's reactions to Kimsey, especially given how largely irrelevant Kimsey had been to his, and AOL's, day-to-day existence for several years. Whether it was a father–son dynamic or not, when Case talked about Kimsey, he didn't sound so much angry as he did hurt, disapproved of.

It was also fascinating to hear Case's reaction to the material about him and his brother Dan. Steve was rankled, understandably, by the suggestion that he could never have made it in business without his fraternal connections. This would upset anyone, especially given what Steve had achieved, and on his own. Likewise, he was offended by the notion that he had some psychic need to surpass his brother.

But when I read Steve the parts about how he and Dan would change the rules of their childhood basketball games—Case Rules— he became more indignant than about anything else. He raised his voice again, nearly to a yell. "That wasn't me and Dan," he said. "That was just Dan. He was the one who changed the rules. Not me."

They had a joke in their own house about Dan changing the rules, he said. Dan was the really competitive one. "I was more `go with the flow.'" Clearly, Steve said, I had misunderstood what his boyhood neighbors had told me. Or maybe they were generalizing about the Case brothers. But they must have really been referring to just Dan, because Steve would never cheat. He said "Gracious in victory, humble in defeat" again. I called back the neighbors to reconfirm. Yes, they assured me, it was both Cases.

When I talked to Dan about this later that Friday, he laughed. Yes, he said, he was definitely more competitive than Steve growing up. He couldn't recall exactly what happened in the basketball games. Mostly, his reaction was, "Who cares?" Long-ago kid stuff, sheesh.

During my reporting, I spoke to Dan Case several times and came to like him a great deal. He was thoughtful, open, didn't take himself too seriously. And—this was unusual for a CEO dealing with a nosy reporter—he was empathetic.

I had an odd personal experience with the Case family as I reported this profile. On my way to visit them in Hawaii, I had to turn back because my wife, Meri, had complications with her pregnancy. Everything turned out to be fine, but it was a scary 48 hours, and I had to cancel all of my scheduled meetings with the Cases in Hawaii. Later that week, I spoke to Dan twice, and he always inquired about how things were with my wife. His parents did, too, as did Bushkin, who was my main point of contact at AOL.

My sit-down with Steve was that week, too. He acknowledged nothing. Not his style. That's OK. Kindness to a demon reporter is hardly a litmus test. Still, it was strange. But also very much in character: Dan the pleaser; Steve too focused for niceties.

Into his adulthood, Dan, ever dutiful, still called his parents every Sunday. Steve e-mailed home when he could. Dan checked in regularly with sister Carin and brother Jeff; Steve, more sporadically. Steve is busy, so they don't want to bother him, Carin said. "I hate to make him feel like we're part of the whirlwind." Steve, she says, has always been his own best friend.

"Steve is my best friend," Dan Case said repeatedly in the course of several conversations. He kept saying, convincingly, that he is thrilled by Steve's success. He joked that the notion of him overshadowing Steve is "not a problem anymore." Yet, I couldn't help wonder how Dan, the golden son, felt about his adult status as the Lower Case of the New Economy.

"Every now and then Dan has to shake his head," their younger brother Jeff told me. "I think he understands this is a strange thing. He realizes this is Steve's time to shine. Maybe he didn't expect it to last this long."

When Steve and Dan attended a White House reception in 1999, people kept coming over and asking Steve to meet some dignitary or cabinet official. It was nonstop, says John Sidgmore, who was there that night. Dan would smile and stand by patiently. Finally, Sidgmore recalls, someone tapped Dan on the shoulder and asked him if he could get Steve's attention. "What am I, your PR person?" Dan said to his brother. "He was kidding," Sidgmore says.

But he seemed, for a split second, exasperated.

CONVERGENCE

Early in 2001, shortly after the AOL–Time Warner merger was ratified, Dan Case was diagnosed with brain cancer.

It was devastating news, especially in high-tech and banking circles, where Dan was quite well liked. He was 43 years old and had four children, one of them an infant. He stepped down as CEO of Hambrecht & Quist in May—he stayed on part-time while receiving radiation treatment. His prognosis was not good.

Through much of 2001, Steve made regular trips to San Francisco to visit Dan and his family. Predictably, friends said he spoke little about Dan's illness. He concentrated on his corporate ambassadorial and philanthropic duties, which he had, by all accounts, eased into comfortably.

He attended a White House meeting on tax policy and a congressional retreat at the Greenbriar resort. He addressed the Council of Americas. He gave a speech urging Latin American leaders to reduce tariffs on high-tech products. He met with the German Deputy Minister. He ate breakfast with the King of

Jordan. He joined George W. Bush for a private White House screening of the HBO film *61**. He pledged $7 million to Punahou School, since rechristened Case Middle School.

He was no longer an insurgent, he was a leader. He was a missionary not for the Internet, but for the notion of "convergence," a single, seamless theater in which cell phones, televisions, computers, personal digital assistants, and whatever else would work together. Internet access and content would be delivered over Time Warner Cable wires and wireless devices. The company would launch a new online service where music from Time Warner artists would be accessible on AOL—just as movies would be available on demand from AOL's network of Web sites. This is what AOL–Time Warner called its destiny of "interlocking dreams."

Several sources at AOL say that Case is not working nearly so hard as he did when he and his unknown firm had so much to prove. He was involved in issues related to getting regulatory approval of the merger, but since remained largely invisible inside the company, except behind podiums. One friend said that post-merger, Case had been as disengaged as Kimsey was in his later years at AOL.

Because he was chairman of the world's biggest media company, Case's speeches were closely watched. His most awaited appearance occurred on May 3, 2001. He addressed Hambrecht & Quist's annual conference, an influential gathering of bankers and technology leaders at San Francisco's Westin St. Francis Hotel.

It became a building curiosity among attendees whether Steve would say anything poignant about the event's host, his brother Dan. Several members of the Case family had come in for the event. This was akin to the valedictory ceremony of Dan Case's career.

Steve, his hair noticeably grayer since the Time Warner deal, stepped to the podium to a standing ovation. It could have gotten sentimental right there. Steve held up his hands. "Times a-tickin, clock's a-wastin,'" he said.

Steve thanked his brother for inviting him. He told a few stories about their boyhood business ventures, about a trip they took to Spain when they were in their early 20s, staying in dingy hotels and drinking a lot of beer. Recently, Steve said, he visited the Spanish president at the presidential palace—and the Spanish president issued them a full pardon for any laws they might have broken. There was some laughter from the crowd. Dan smiled. There was a pause. Maybe it would get sentimental now. But then Steve Case launched into his prepared remarks, about convergence or something, and he was on to the next thing.

EPILOGUE

Ｏne of the problems with writing a book about technology is that a terrifying qualifier looms over the whole process:

"Everything can change."

And it probably will, several times over. Or maybe everything already *has* changed, weeks ago, in some secret deal, basement invention or late-night cubicle brainstorm: The flash of inspiration that makes Cisco's routers unnecessary; the court ruling that slices Microsoft in half; the hand-held shopping gadget that banishes Amazon to yesterday; the surfing, biking, boating, or flying calamity that kills Larry Ellison.

Yikes. In the same way that engineers live in fear of their inventions getting "obsoleted" (one of those Silicon Valley words), nothing begs for irrelevance more than a plodding, static, "old media" outlet like a book. When I started working on this project, in February 2000, the Internet stock bubble was nearing its peak. People would speak of the "New Economy" as a normal and permanent fact of modern life, with no allowance for the possibility that it could, in fact, get old. Wall Street was punishing AOL for "selling out" its sexy, Internet-only allure for Time-Warner's tradition and stability. Jeff Bezos had just been named Time's Man of the Year. John Chambers was being called high-tech's best CEO and Cisco was primed to become Wall Street's most valuable company. Larry Ellison was saying that Oracle's vital-to-the-Internet software was in the process of "obsoleting" Microsoft's PC-oriented software. Microsoft seemed battered, vulnerable and adrift, confronted with a host of emboldened competitors, a bitter loss in federal court and the exodus of key executives. Gates, who had just reliquished his CEO's job, seemed to be easing into a state of semi-retirement.

That was 18 months ago.

Today, Microsoft is as much a powerhouse as ever with its unveiling of the XP operating system, its most awaited product in years, whose creation was supervised closely by the still-Richest Man in the World. The company is locked in a Cold War with AOL for control of your media life—from desktop, to set-top, to content offerings. And few would call Steve Case's move to buy Time-Warner a sellout today. Far from it, the acquisition could go down as the single best strategic move of this commercial era, a decision that protected AOL from the bubble-bursting damage that's befallen Oracle, Cisco, Amazon—all of whom have lost considerable luster since I began this project.

In other words, from February 2000 to September 2001, everything has changed.

Or has it?

Yes, the Nasdaq has landed, the U.S. economy has, too, and the imperative of world domination has been replaced by the virtue of at-home execution. (To say nothing of a nation suddenly preoccupied with fighting a war.) But Gates, Case, Chambers, Bezos and Ellison still all preside over the franchise firms in a cultural and economic world that they have changed forever—and that has changed them forever. Their stock prices and profits might dip, but none of these companies is close to losing their strangleholds on the sectors with which they've become synonomous. Many of their competitors have struggled much worse than they have.

This is not to say the New Imperialists don't all face major challenges and big questions. Gates' professional future remains clouded by the still-uncertain resolution of the government's antitrust case. Ellison is dangerously alone at the top of Oracle, having lost another generation of top executives (Executive Vice President Gary Bloom quit a few months after Ray Lane did). His company—which relies on companies paying large sums for its sophisticated software tools—is vulnerable to the kinds of captial spending slowdowns that have occurred in 2001; the same slump that's hampered Cisco and which continues to make John Chambers so uncharacteristically beleaguered. Can Chambers lead in an extended downturn? Those answers are unfolding, too.

The biggest questions surround Amazon: on one hand, not only have its e-commerce rival stumbled, most of them have closed. But on the other hand, Amazon's ability to stay solvent long enough to profit from its singular position remains very much unknown. Amazon has lost money for 17 consecutive quarters. Its cash reserves at the end of the second quarter of 2001 were $161 million, down from $251 million in the first quarter. Bezos became a relatively scarce figure in the summer of 2001, lowering his once sky-high profile in the media, even in the Amazon hallways, according to a company source.

Will Amazon "make it?" My guess is yes, if not by the handiwork of Bezos' brainiacs, then perhaps as a logical acquisition target for a large media or retail firm such as Bertelsmann or AOL (which made a $100 million investment, in Amazon in July). Either way, it's likely that in five years, people will still be buying from some virtual iteration of Amazon—and, Bezos will still be laughing, somewhere, his place in the mythology of this weird time assured. Again, that's just a guess, rendered with the standing caveat.

Everything can change.

What makes these men different? What qualities set them apart? I have been asked variations on this repeatedly since I began this enterprise. The connective tissue questions. Surely, I have formed some theory on why Gates, Case, Ellison, Bezos and Chambers could succeed so stunningly while others could not, right? But while it was not for lack of agonizing on my part, my answers were always equivocal. Let's see: they are all driven, smart and very, very, lucky. Their identities, public and private, are tied wholly to the fates of their enterprises, fates have teetered on the fine line between hope and hubris that these men have straddled throughout their lives.

They owned enough self-confidence to believe they deserved to be "anywhere," to put a computer on every desktop, to get big fast, to "empower" the Internet generation. Somehow, they were wired, or programmed, to jump as boldly as they did into one of the great open spaces in commercial history. Digital space, a sprawling outlet where they could forge industries and also identities.

Where Gates could go from lonely prodigy to the world's prodigy. Where Ellison could go from unbridled youth to unbridled multi-billionaire. Where John Chambers could re-focus his ambitions from the old corporate ladder to a new corporate frontier. Where Steve Case could hang around, endure, not be reined in and make his own rules. Where Jeff Bezos could do something memorable.

Where they could all be in charge.

The New Imperialists are linked in history, united in a club of wealth, power, influence and celebrity few of us will ever join, let alone identify with. But rather than impose too much order on their stories and selves, I wanted to let their gifts and frailties to stand as discreetly as possible, as individual lives, five stories for these times. We can leave the rest to history, and the future to them.

INDEX

A